You've Lost Your Mind
Now Find Your Soul

A Human's Path to Awakening

Rev. Dr. Sandy Range, Ph.D. LMHC

BALBOA
PRESS
A DIVISION OF HAY HOUSE

Copyright © 2019 Rev. Dr. Sandy Range, Ph.D. LMHC.

All rights reserved. No part of this book may be used or reproduced by any means, graphic, electronic, or mechanical, including photocopying, recording, taping or by any information storage retrieval system without the written permission of the author except in the case of brief quotations embodied in critical articles and reviews.

Balboa Press books may be ordered through booksellers or by contacting:

Balboa Press
A Division of Hay House
1663 Liberty Drive
Bloomington, IN 47403
www.balboapress.com
1 (877) 407-4847

Because of the dynamic nature of the Internet, any web addresses or links contained in this book may have changed since publication and may no longer be valid. The views expressed in this work are solely those of the author and do not necessarily reflect the views of the publisher, and the publisher hereby disclaims any responsibility for them.

The author of this book does not dispense medical advice or prescribe the use of any technique as a form of treatment for physical, emotional, or medical problems without the advice of a physician, either directly or indirectly. The intent of the author is only to offer information of a general nature to help you in your quest for emotional and spiritual well-being. In the event you use any of the information in this book for yourself, which is your constitutional right, the author and the publisher assume no responsibility for your actions.

Any people depicted in stock imagery provided by Getty Images are models, and such images are being used for illustrative purposes only. Certain stock imagery © Getty Images.

Scripture quotations marked KJV are from the Holy Bible, King James Version (Authorized Version). First published in 1611. Quoted from the KJV Classic Reference Bible, Copyright © 1983 by Zondervan Corporation.

Print information available on the last page.

ISBN: 978-1-9822-3159-0 (sc)
ISBN: 978-1-9822-3158-3 (hc)
ISBN: 978-1-9822-3162-0 (e)

Library of Congress Control Number: 2019910004

Balboa Press rev. date: 07/19/2019

ACKNOWLEDGMENTS

This book would not have been written, or should I say completed without the inspiration and guidance from my Ascended Alliance of Universal Intelligences, and the patrons, patients and clients of Intentional Self, LLC. To all of you my heart-felt thanks.

To my supervisees, my friends, my colleagues throughout my life and the countless clients that I have had the opportunity to not only serve, but to learn from as well. I thank you from the bottom of my heart.

To my family: My son David, my sister Tonia, and my brother Jeff. I love you all so very much. Without you I would never have become the person I am today: Growth & evolution!

To my sweet mother Mary Elizabeth. I hope you are soaring the universe in light and love. I know you are my guiding angel, my inspiration and my muse. It may have taken some time, but you have taught me well. I love you so much and I miss you. Thank you mom!

To my dad, Samuel Mason. You just left us as I was writing the last two chapters of this book. You have just transitioned and I was your departing doula, calling the ancestors to guide you and heal you on your journey. Be blessed daddy. Now you are whole again.

Of course, I have to give props to Keith Ogorek of Balboa Press and the ALC and CEO, Reid Tracy of Hay House Publishing who both provided me guidance each step of the way right through to completion of this book! Thank you from my soul!

CONTENTS

Introduction xi

Part 1: This is Your Why!

Chapter 1	The Goal is Your Soul 1
Chapter 2	Mindfulness Gives Sight 13
Chapter 3	The Ego: Who Are You Anyway? 19
Chapter 4	Higher Intelligence – Divine mind 35
Chapter 5	The Bible or Fake News? 45
Chapter 6	The Christ Being 61
Chapter 7	The Road to Transformation 79
Chapter 8	Your Intentional Self 93
Chapter 9	Authenticity 101
Chapter 10	Meaning Making 107
Chapter 11	Your Mental and Physical Wellness 113
Chapter 12	The Ancestors 123

Part 2: Finding Your Soul after You Lose Your Mind!

Chapter 13	(C1) How Do I Find My Soul? 133
Chapter 14	(C2) About Being Mindful and How! 141
Chapter 15	(C3) How Do I Get Rid of Ego? 151
Chapter 16	(C4) Higher Mind to Divine mind 159

Chapter 17 (C7) The Road to Transformation 163
Chapter 18 (C9) I Thought I was Already Authentic! 169
Chapter 19 (C10): Finding the Meaning.................................. 175
Chapter 20 (C11) Healthy Habits Maintained 179
Chapter 21 (C12) The Ancestor Connection............................ 185

Part 3: Your Beginning

Chapter 22 This is the Beginning 191
Chapter 23 You are the Universe. The Universe is You 199

Resources 215
Works Cited 221
Appendix 225

INTRODUCTION

This book was written for everyone who desires to elevate his or her condition to a status of joy in every aspect of your life: mentally, emotionally, socially, professionally, relationally, financially and especially spiritually. This book was specifically written for disadvantaged people of color of all nationalities and other marginalized groups, but this information is for all people regardless of where you come from or the color of your skin. The purpose of this writing is to show people how to elevate in consciousness and live a soulful life guided by Divine mind to elevate ourselves, our societies and the world.

The title was derived from a quote by John Muir who stated, *"And into the forest I go, to lose my mind and find my soul."* So, in order to find your soul you must first lose your mind. You will find out what this means in the content of this book. What is different about this book is that I am sharing with each of you the so-called secrets, processes and methods used by Spirit to elevate your consciousness to a state of Divinity. In this state you are able to achieve almost anything that is in your highest good.

So, who is Rev. Dr. Sandy Range and why did I write this book? Professionally, I am a Licensed Psychotherapist in Massachusetts, Certified Hypnotherapist, Certified Trauma Specialist and Ordained Metaphysical Minister, Medicine Woman and Shaman. I won't bore you with the countless certifications I have received throughout my many decades of doing this work. With much intense introspection of wanting to reach more people and affect more lives, I blossomed from my cocoon and transformed myself to become the Self I Intended to Be: Soul!

For most of my adult life I just worked a regular job. Night shifts, day shifts and everything in between. There was a time I spent ten years working with homeless women and found my calling by counseling and running groups for these women to help them build confidence and esteem and open their minds to abundance (even though I was still working on my own abundance). Although there were a few who used this information to get out of the shelters, I found out that there was so much internal damage due to abuse, trauma, drug use and mental illness that the information and guidance I provided wasn't easily understood, never mind being absorbed and utilized. I was in my forties when I went back to school for my Master's degree in psychology. In my sixties I received my doctorate in Esoteric Theology. Mental, Emotional and Spiritual counseling was my new love. I still practice today. Then came a realization. I would never truly know what I was meant for or my true purpose in this life unless I took myself a few steps further.

I embarked on a journey of self-mastery and success making. I studied the various teachers and gurus for self-development. I attended countless workshops and seminars. I engaged in business partnerships and had a couple of multi-level marketing businesses. I had plenty of success, but always lost it all. I've been through bankruptcy, had the bill collectors calling my home and yes, I've been homeless too. At a few points in my life didn't know where my next meal would come from. I had so many losses I almost felt defeated. I began to tell myself (dis-empowering programming) that being successful or knowing my purpose must not be in my calling and that I'm probably destined to remain poor and at a loss. I'll bet you've had these same thoughts many times over!

I came from very humble beginnings like many of you. I was born the second daughter of my nurse mother and my police officer father. My parents divorced when I was five years old and my sister ten. I loved both of my parents, but as a child I didn't spend much time with either of them or my sister. I was always being shipped off to my maternal grandmother's house. It wasn't until much later in life did I find out that it was for my own protection, but as a small child I didn't see it that way. I believed they didn't really want me around. I knew my sister didn't. I found out later in life that she hated the fact that I was born and continued to let me know this throughout my entire life – not verbally, but behaviorally. Of course, this wasn't her fault either. It was the result of how she was treated and the trauma she faced. I felt neglected, disowned, and unwanted. I never even remembered receiving a hug or kiss from the adults around me, but I remember being sexually molested as a child by a neighbor; scared nearly to death on a daily basis at the expense of my uncle's fun (he was only 9 years older than me); and not understanding why all my aunts and uncles never wanted me around. Although I had a dozen cousins I never became close to any of them, yet all the rest of them were very close. Because of that I learned nothing about positive, healthy relationships although I yearned for them each and every day. Talk about damaged!

The other thing I never learned was how to be fiscally responsible. My parents always struggled financially and after their divorce we left our house in Jamaica Plain and my mom moved my sister and me into a small, cold third floor apartment. With her menial nurse's salary she was barely able to pay the bills and keep me and my sister with food and clothes. She sacrificed a lot (sacrifice – something else I learned how to do very well). She worked double shifts multiple nights a week. I still never got to spend any time with her and now, dad was gone too. My parents modeled behaviors of struggle and strife, but it was not their fault either. They learned what they knew from the modeled behaviors of their parents, peers and society. This is a sad reality how poverty, stress and struggle is passed down from generation to generation, especially for people of color and marginalized groups. This is not to say that every disadvantaged family experiences this kind of financial stress, but those that "made it" had something the rest of us did not. We will discuss this a little later.

Unfortunately, for many disadvantaged people and People of Color, the culture of mainstream society had its way of forcing upon us feelings of inadequacy, insecurities and poor self-esteem. Throughout history, in these United States, racism, discrimination and abuse played enormous roles in keeping people poor, lacking confidence, feeling insecure and afraid for our lives, literally.

I grew up in the 1950's, 60's and 70's. These were decades belonging to Jim Crow, the Civil Rights Movement, the Viet Nam war, and the flower power of the Hippie Movement. It was a time of great change. New freedoms for African Americans, women and even a new acknowledgement for the freedoms and treaty rights of Native Americans were born (but not realized). But during these times the energy of the country split into thirds. Yes, Thirds!

1) After the Viet Nam war soldiers returned to a country that was not prepared to receive them with the dignity they deserved. It was an ugly war that many people thought we should never have fought. Still for the young soldiers who did fight, coming home to America was devastating for many. Post Traumatic Stress Disorder combined with the lack of jobs and a country that treated them like second class citizens forced many returning vets into homelessness, drugs, alcohol, and suicide. During the 1980's and 1990's was a time when state mental hospitals closed down and thousands of mentally ill and unstable people were turned into the streets, literally (this caused the rise of the shelter industry). This period created a population of extremely poor, destitute and dysfunctional people.

2) After the Hippie Movement came Young Urban Professionals (Yuppies). These were former hippies who cleaned up their acts at the request and often financial bribery of their

parents. Near the end of the Hippie Movement in the 1970's and 1980's and with the breakthrough of newer, faster, more intelligent technology (Personal Computers) many hippies who were the rebellious children of very affluent families, took advantage of the deals made with their parents. Their parents paid for them to go back to college and complete their degrees, put them into businesses or used their influence to obtain well-paying corporate careers. I'm not saying every hippie had this opportunity, but so many did!

There were the Black Urban Professionals (Buppies) who were able to land lucrative jobs in corporations as well. Because of the strides made from the Civil Rights Movement (Equal Rights), Black Power, and the Hippie Movement many companies, by law, had to begin hiring qualified minorities, but this also sparked anger from mainstream society as many of these careers for minorities came through Affirmative Action. In the late 1970's and early 1980's these people became the new middle class. A middle class that was very well off (although not wealthy).

3) Also during this era, with an increase of full force intensity, there was "Welfare." This was a lifesaver for the poorest of the poor, especially children. It was a way for poor families to support themselves. It was and still is both a blessing and a curse. After the Great Depression of 1929, the federal government got involved and welfare transformed. It was meant to be a temporary assistance to get people back on their feet. Back then, welfare expenditures were about 0.2 percent. From the 1980's into the 21st century expenditures soared to 4 percent. This does not include health care for the poor. While welfare was and is a saving grace for the poor of all races and nationalities it also became a crutch for many. It was free, easy money (though not very much). It made paupers of people with potential. It allowed people to become dependent on it. It was a trap of dependency: a

new disability. People became welfare disabled. For many, a monthly welfare check was expected and if it was late people got angry and felt entitled. Now, the law limits lifetime welfare assistance according to which state you live in and requires most able-bodied adults to work after two years on welfare. In Massachusetts there is a lifetime benefit, but you must follow certain guidelines, take advantage of job training (if needed) and find work. Still some recipients are angered that their benefits are only temporary, and during the few years of supplemental help, many do not take advantage of ways to become independent and sprint the path towards independence and abundance. What does this say about our consciousness?

So here we have three distinct populations of people. The mentally disabled and homeless, the shrinking and unstable middle class and the welfare disabled. None of these people need suffer the pangs of poverty and lack except if one chooses to do so. Yes! I said it…choose!

You already have inside of you everything you need to be successful and create abundance in every aspect of your life. I refer to abundance being not just monetary. It occurs mentally, emotionally, spiritually, physically, financially, socially and professionally at least while still on planet Earth.

The chapters in this book will describe what is needed and what you must do to become intentional in every aspect of your Being in order to become your true Soul Self. Abundance is a holistic process. If you are serious you will take to heart every single word because we are about to get deep. You have a lot of soul searching and healing to do and a lot of deep inner work must be done. This is a holistic approach to becoming the person you intend to be according to each person's truth. You will also read about my own life lessons and my spiritual, emotional and mental growth and evolution. Some of the lessons were quite difficult, others easy peasy, but all very important and significant lessons. The key is to recognize and acknowledge the lessons when they present themselves.

What you may also not realize is that abundance is everything spiritual. Spirituality is not religion. In order to reach the pinnacle of our true selves we must first know who we are. Most of us do not. It may surprise you!

I have placed daily practices at the end of this book that you should complete in order to move through what is keeping you stuck in your condition. It's quite simple, but it is not easy. Some of you will read every word and apply all the teachings in this text. Some of you will attend one of our transformational webinars or workshops or receive personalized counseling or coaching from us or elsewhere. You will go on to achieve the goal. For those of you that do, all I ask is that you teach others to do the same. "Each one, teach one." Give them a copy of this book. It is time to lift all of us up out of despair and into a permanent state of truth in mind, body and spirit that we can pass down to our children and our children's children. Teach others, especially our children, to rise to levels of higher consciousness and spiritual knowing with you. Let us stop the cycle we have been forced into.

For those of you that feel this may be too hard to do. All I ask of you is to read this book. Come back to it later, but not too far in the future. Working through your inner stuff, the stuff that keeps you stuck, is hard and you might give up, but are you satisfied with your current status in life? If you are truly tired of your condition, tired of being sick and tired, give it a chance and do the work. Follow the lessons in this book and you won't be affected by any negativity that may come along. You will find yourself in a position that will afford you and your loved ones a very peaceful, loving and fulfilling life.

When you become a spiritually awake person you stimulate the economy and society as a whole. Imagine if everyone who is poor changed their mind, changed their condition and became a shareholder in Divine knowledge. One of the rules is to share the knowledge with others and at least plant seeds. Not everyone will be ready to transform. This is very different from what mainstream society does, except with their own. What is also required is to immerse yourself in transformation mentally, emotionally, spiritually and physically. This is a holistic process.

You have within you everything you need to transform and awaken to your purpose. You have a mind (thought), a heart (love-mind) and spirit. (Divine will) That's all it takes. Let's begin shall we?

Remember, you already have within you everything you need to be great! Now, be INSPIRED!
Dr. Sandy Range

PART ONE

THIS IS YOUR WHY!

> "When you develop your inner power, your confidence, your sense of peace, no matter what anyone does, or says they cannot disturb you, interrupt you or change you. You hold the power!"
> Dr. Sandy Range

CHAPTER ONE

The Goal is Your Soul

You need to know that change is inevitable.

Now, the first thing you need to know before you embark on this reading is that this book is not just about material abundance. That is a side effect that can happen. What you need to know is abundance is a holistic concept. This means that you will learn how to manifest what you need in your life, but through a holistic practice of learning, understanding and incorporating your divine knowledge and your soul knowing. Unless and until we truly understand our own divinity we will forever be in a spiral of confusion and suffering. And no, this is not about religion.

The goal of this book and process is to help you purge the energetic density of your physical being and your brain-mind consciousness and re-align with your true self, to become, once again, connected as *one* with Divine mind. Divine mind is a universal consciousness. The likes of Issa/Jesus, Buddha, St Germaine, Mani, Mary Magdalena (yes, that's right), Quan Yin, Gandhi, the Dalai Lama and many other great and knowledgeable spiritual leaders all possessed Divine mind. In other words, like them, you need to find your soul!

We need to begin to purge what is no longer useful intentionally. Being intentional is being deliberate and purposeful. When we are intentional with our thoughts and words we are better understood. When we are intentional with our actions we accomplish more. When we are intentional with our behaviors we show our true selves. Being intentional in all we do is a way of showing that we are present and aware of ourselves and the world around us, including the spirit world. How are you living your life?

One of the first steps to becoming intentional is to recognize and acknowledge our spirit or soul self. That is our true self! The self we have forgotten. More on intention in chapter eight. To go from where we are now to becoming our true selves we first must go through a transformation. Transformation comes in all sizes, shapes and packages. Sometimes it feels good and sometimes it doesn't. You may often wonder when change comes to push or shove, are you being receptive or are you holding your ground and fighting against it?

What usually happens is that we, initially, don't realize that change is happening. Most of us don't. All we're thinking is that something is standing in our way. That some force is keeping us from our agendas! We start checking to see what is going *wrong* and looking for ways to rectify the situation.

When change comes it usually comes in the form of a gentle nudge. That is the *force* that appears to get in the way. When we push back or fight the flow of change, change will stand its ground and dig in its heels so to speak. We usually push back even harder making every attempt to make things work the way we desire. Change says, "No you don't buddy! Open your eyes. Listen to me. I'm trying to help you along here."

Change can come in the form of a person, a situation, a condition, an experience and a whole lot more. Change comes to transform us. It comes to make us better at who we are and what we do. It comes when we are weary, tired, overworked, overwhelmed, stuck, depressed, sad, anxious, confused, angry, ego driven, and just plain dumbfounded!

Resisting change is like walking down a wooded path. You come to a fork in the road. There is a huge fallen tree on one path and a clear way on the opposite path. Our human agenda says to climb over that fallen tree because *my goal is down that road and that's where I want to go.* You may climb over it, but change will keep placing more trees, brush, rocks and debris in your way until you realize that you can go no farther. You have to stop. Change will force us, tattered and worn from our attempts, to go back to the fork and follow the clear path change has laid out for us, that is, if we are open and receptive enough to realize it. Ego, can trip us up at times like this. Many of us continue down that cluttered path with nowhere to go. What happens? We get disillusioned. We feel we will never accomplish our dreams and goals. Some of us give up entirely.

So, when change comes and starts pushing you around, stop yourself and take notice. Realize that when your agenda is not being fulfilled no matter how hard you try, there is a reason for it. Pay attention! So, when this happens, and it has happened and will continue to happen, try the following:

Stop pushing so hard and stop trying to figure out what's wrong. Nothing is wrong. This is a time to take sanctuary. Go to your quiet place and think upon your methods for achieving your desired results. At times you may have to just stop what you are doing for a day or two, and maybe longer. Sometimes we just have to let go and let God! But that doesn't mean to stop taking action. God helps those who help themselves! It means, allowing the answers to come freely.

We each are connected to a higher intelligence. Tapping into that intelligence is fairly easy. Just wait and listen., don't push for an answer. The answer is always there. It always comes. It may not be the answer we are looking for, but it is usually the right answer. It may take us in a different or new direction. It may cause us to re-evaluate relationships or business goals. It may make us take stock of what we truly desire to accomplish. It may cause us to just be more aware of our surroundings and to make necessary changes in our environment.

Awareness of when change comes is key to saving yourself a lot of time and anguish! If whatever you are doing is not working the way you intend, change is knocking at your door to transform you or your agenda. It is always for the better and always for good!

When you follow that still small voice of change from your higher intelligence, it feels good, it feels right. You know the direction you need to take. Follow it! Still, you may need to make adjustments along the way. When you allow your habitual patterns to interfere with the vision change has for you it will push you to the brink to make you the best you can or you may fail miserably! Avoid the "shove" that change will force upon you. Stop, wait, listen, and then do. Be consciously aware of challenges that seem to pop up and know when ego is getting in the way!

I remember wanting to open an In Home Therapy (IHT) and private counseling clinic not so long ago. I found a great location and the perfect rent. I spent more than a year formulating policy and procedure manuals, employee handbooks, the appropriate guidelines and documents we would need to use, along with making sure the two regulatory agencies that would grant me the appropriate certifications and licensure for a clinic were satisfied. They cost a pretty sum too. I paid for all this including furnishings, equipment and supplies out of my pocket.

The more I insisted this was the right thing to do, the more I became overwhelmed, irritable, anxious and not so nice to the people I had working to help me open this clinic. While I received wonderful feedback for the work I had put in and received one certification from the Joint Commission, the licensing agency, the Department of Public Health, refused to provide the license due to not having a handicapped bathroom. Since I rented this unit, I was not able to redesign the bathroom to accommodate handicapped accessibility. Now, I had left my job and had no more income. What was I to do? I had an epiphany! I suddenly realized that this venture was turning me into someone I was not. Not to mention the signs along the way during that year that I thought were mere distractions, including the severe delays for the inspections from DPH that put me over the one-year mark for opening at a cost from my own wallet.

I realized that I had become a tyrant (ego). At least that's how I saw myself. I returned to the meditation practice that I had not practiced during the entire time of preparation. I saw where I had made my mistakes and acknowledged where and when change had come to nudge and then pushed me into a new direction. I made the change down the path of least resistance and I am happier for it and more prosperous too. But I didn't see change when it first came to nudge!

Learn to become your Intentional Self! A holistic coach, counselor or psychotherapist might help you define, mold and carry out your vision for success and hold you accountable until you reach your desired results. If you suffer from depression, anxiety, trauma or something else please seek help so that you can clear out those negative and debilitating emotional influences and make way for clarity, balance and positive energy.

How many of us discount our own spiritual powers? These innate gifts are within each of us. Maybe you have the gifts of healing, channeling or transmission, telepathy, prophecy, knowledge, compassion, music, teaching, art or dance. Or maybe you're are a math genius or a scientist or have ideas for growing organic foods or to help the environment, and so much more. These gifts are not just for the so-called "chosen" although it does take some inner work and practice to allow your gifts to surface and know what to do with them.

When I was younger my mother knew I had Spiritual gifts and she tried to promote my spiritual powers at every turn. As a child and into my teens I was adept at seeing. I was a seer. I just knew what was coming, but especially could read clearly and accurately into others.

I also had the "touch." I was able to help others heal emotionally and spiritually through my laying on of hands. Of course, once people are healed spiritually they also begin to heal physically! However, in childhood I looked upon these gifts as 'just the way things are.' To me they did not seem special or rather, I did not have an ego attachment to them. In fact I wondered why my friends and other adults would ask me very specific questions about their lives and be truly interested in what I had to say. Others would have me touch them on the shoulders or head and claim a sense of rejuvenation and healing! The word spread, but I had no conscious idea what I was accomplishing.

In my early adulthood I wandered away from my gifts and completely ignored them. I was still able to see, but life circumstances happened and I stopped trusting myself. It wasn't until a few decades later, when I had a second calling, that I began my own healing and became devout in my meditations and esoteric practices again! Now, it's not an easy path, but it is simple to follow. You must heal yourself first, learn and practice awareness, and live your life in a Divine manner (you are divine after all)! Then you can practice, with the right guide or teacher, to open to your innate gifts and use them to heal others and the planet!

What I'm sharing with you is that you have great Spiritual power! You can tap into and use your spiritual powers for the good of yourself, others, even the world! Think about what your gifts might be. Maybe you already know, maybe you too don't trust your gifts or maybe you think you have none at all! You do! If you would like help in accessing your Spiritual Gifts, contact us. We can counsel you and guide you to open to your power!

Change is good. It is also inevitable. Don't fight against change. It comes to teach us. To help us learn, grow and evolve. Yes, it is sometimes painful, but remember the wooded path. Will you fight through the fallen trees and rocks? Or will you take the clear, narrow, but curvy path?

We all face problems in our lives. It's helpful to look at problems as challenges. A challenge is like a contest. It is something we can overcome or win. When we look at problems and become disillusioned, overwhelmed, depressed, angry, the problem appears to get even bigger and more disturbing and daunting. It overwhelms us and we can feel defeated. A challenge, on the other hand, can provide us confidence, alertness, and the will to win. However, winning is not the goal of problems or challenges as that attitude belongs to ego. Challenges present themselves to help us grow. There is always a lesson or teaching within the presented challenge.

Hindsight is a very useful tool. When we look back at old challenges that we have come through, try to figure out what the lesson was. Attempt to see what you've learned and how you've grown (if so). Even the most difficult and painful challenges have a lesson within them. When we are seeking clarity about the lesson it is never a good idea to place blame outside of yourself. Hear me out!

As a psychotherapist and a trauma specialist I have heard many heart wrenching stories of sexual, physical, emotional and verbal abuse and neglect. I've heard stories of war time trauma, natural disasters, horrible accidents, homicides and suicides. In some of these cases it was at the hands of another that caused the trauma. The victim is never blamed. However, what I am getting at is taking that traumatic incident (unless you have not yet dealt with your trauma) and seeing how you have come through it all. There was something within you that helped you to survive. There was a strength, a skill, a resilience or a knowing that helped you through it. When I say to not place blame outside of yourself, that is the point of hindsight: to see what it is you possess within that helped you to grow and evolve from the challenge.

It is also, and this may be hard to hear, an opportunity to see your part in the victimization. Why were you in the wrong place at the wrong time? Were you teasing or taunting someone? Were you thinking negative thoughts about someone or something else?

Were you wishing something bad to happen to someone else? Were you trying to get revenge? Were you pitying yourself? Were you trying to make something happen or someone fall in love with you? Maybe you were trying to actually hurt someone or gain someone's affection! You get the idea now. We are always looking to place blame outside of ourselves.

There is, however, another reason bad things happen to us. Before we are born we have the opportunity to choose what family, what society, what culture, what nation we will be born into. We also gain knowledge of what kind of life we will live. Sometimes, a soul will choose a very hard life or to be born with some disability to grow and evolve more rapidly. Sometimes a soul will choose a life that is relatively easy peasy as a break on our sojourn and evolution as human souls.

Unfortunately, because we are all born with a veil of forgetfulness, we do not remember what the goal was exactly. However, as very young children we still have that knowing present within us. It is our parents/caregivers, teachers, peers that lead us away from our spiritual knowings into a state of worldly being, sensory overload and forgetfulness. Let us think about this for a moment. Do you remember being very young and playful with a mind full to the brim of imaginings and fantasies that brought you pleasure? Maybe you had an imaginary friend or two or three? Could you see the world with eyes that were big and bright? Did you know things of other worldly natures (although maybe not realize exactly what it was)? I could go on and on with examples, but think on these things for a moment or more.

What happens to us as young children is that once we reach a certain age, our caregivers begin telling us to stop! Stop imagining things! Stop daydreaming. Stop being silly! Stop, Stop Stop! Goodness forbid if we had imaginary friends beyond a certain age. Then we are sent to psychologists and therapists and diagnosed and treated to help us get rid of these imaginary friends. Yikes! Do we now have some early onset psychosis? That's what they would have us think. As a child, we are beaten down emotionally, mentally and especially spiritually! We have no choice, but to conform and rid ourselves of our spiritual knowing and communications. If by chance we hold on to some of our gifts, as we get older, teachers and peers start telling us we are weird or different. They shun us or make fun of us. Sometimes we are even bullied.

Children that cannot remember any of their spirituality, most likely had caregivers that were either uncaring, neglectful or hurtful toward us. Maybe we were traumatized at a very young age. If this is you, don't worry. Your spiritual insights and powers have never left you. In fact they helped you to get through it all and be the person you are today. Damage? Maybe, but you are not defeated! In fact your trauma may actually be a blessings with a little help from a knowledgeable, holistic therapist.

I want to address parents and caregivers of young children. If you are reading this book, you are looking to enlighten your mind and become connected to the Source of All That Is. Do not leave your children behind. Encourage their fantastical meanderings, their imaginings, their invisible friends. Talk to your children when they are in fantasy mode. Ask them who they are talking to and what is going on. Let them know it's okay for them to fantasize and encourage their imaginations. Teach them to remember who they are while they are so new on this planet.

I will talk about methods for daily practice to connect once again to our spirituality and achieve Divine mind. Do not leave your children out of those practices. Make sure they too engage in those practices.

Now, a lot of people may think they need to close themselves in while doing this work. We might believe that the only way we can practice our spirituality is to remove ourselves from the world. Thinking about life and the situation this county is in today, I tried to separate myself, energetically, from the negativity that surrounds me. I prayed a lot. I meditated a lot. I attempted to be at peace wherever I went. I was mindful that I am keeping an open mind and practicing acceptance. I tried to not watch the news. In keeping with my quest for an enlightened consciousness I wondered if I was being too distant from the reality of the world.

A relative once said to me, "I'd come to visit more often if you weren't being such a recluse." He was right! I'd go to my office to see clients and patients. I'd work on my writings and my papers, I'd facilitate my groups and workshops then I'd go home to my sanctuary. I rarely took phone calls on my down time and I'd rarely go out with friends.

I was happy like that. In my bliss! Actually, however, that comment woke me up to a realization that an enlightened mind doesn't remove itself from the realities of this world. It engages in it. By engaging one is put to the test of true enlightenment. Monks will often go out into the world alone with nothing except what is on their backs and live that way for years at a time, depending on the charity of others for food and clothing. We probably can't do that in the country and culture we live in today, but you get my meaning don't you?

If we can be at peace, be accepting of others as they are, continually be in a state of mindful meditation, and not be disturbed, angered or put off by our surroundings or society then we achieve enlightenment. It is being in the world, but not of the world.

However, enlightenment does not mean complacency. It does not mean ignoring reality or hiding from the truth of this world. An enlightened mind does what it can to help. It does more than pray and meditate and hope. An enlightened mind, keeping balanced and mindful, goes into the trenches. It engages people and discovers the causes of their pain. Enlightenment can be contagious if we are truly filled with the Light in enlightenment.

We truly do create our own realities by how we perceive the world around us. If we see only horror, pain and suffering and that is where we dwell mentally, our reality becomes one of the same energy. Enlightened minds are able to fight the good fight without becoming entrenched or attached to the event or the outcome. We do what needs to be done and let it go.

So think upon this as you embark on your own spiritual journey.

*We are all Divine Beings.
We are all walking this earth
clothed in flesh that weighs us down
mentally, physically and most importantly, spiritually.
It is time to recognize who and what we are.
Know your divinity and act accordingly.*
Dr. Sandy Range

CHAPTER TWO

Mindfulness Gives Sight

All we see in the mainstream news media these days is violence, political and corporate corruption, war and mayhem around the world. These images and thought forms being created and forced upon us tend to cause a state of hypnosis among the masses of people around the world. We believe what we see without question and we fall prey to a consciousness of mistrust, doubt, anger, and pain. We believe, without question, that even our neighbors may be terrorists, gangsters or criminals out to cause us harm. We become paranoid, and in severe cases, delusional. We are so mistrusting of others that we actually believe we are always unsafe and have a need to find and incriminate an innocent bystander and protect ourselves in extraordinarily nonsensical ways.

Now, I'm not saying there is no real corruption in our society. There definitely is. What I am saying is we need NOT to take things at face value. There is always a root cause and that cause may not be exactly what we've been told. Our governments have a way of *protecting us from the truth*. In actuality they are simply hiding the truth to which we would all probably disagree with. In many cases it is our own leaders who have duped us with policies signed under the table, meaning there was no media coverage until the signing was over and applied to the government's citizens. It is us, the people, who reap the rewards or penalties.

I am concerned about the world. I am concerned about my Nation, I am concerned about my home state of Massachusetts and my community. I am concerned that this Nation is falling behind the rest of the world. I am concerned that we are so asleep that we will be the cause of our beautiful Nation, every living forest and its creatures; our ecosystem and our environment, to be destroyed, by one person at a time.

Look around you. Better yet, look up. Look up at the sky and tell me what you see. What are those long lasting streaks in the sky? Look at your food. What do you see? What do those numbers on your fruits and vegetables mean and why are we eager to consume them without finding out (see Resources)? We have an overabundance of genetically modified and genetically engineered foods that include both plants and animals: almost every animal bred and all factory farmed animals for human consumption. We have more sickness, debilitating diseases, and death than ever before. Why? Could it be those GM and GE foods? Hmmm! All I'm asking is that you do your research. Stay healthy or get healthy. You can do this on your own. You will know when you need to see a doctor.

What we do not see in the world is the shift that is happening. Mainstream news media won't publicize the good that is happening. It won't allow us to see the changes being made all over the world. It is not newsworthy to show us the millions of people who have had a shift and a raising of their consciousness' to make real change for good. Is it only our Nation, the good ol' USA that is asleep? We may not be the only Nation, but we are certainly one of the largest and most powerful Nations that are just sleepwalking into our destruction? This can cause a residual effect around the world and at the very least on our own continent. How many species of animals have already gone extinct in our lifetime? Too many, and we may be next over the next few generations if we're not very, very careful.

I am asking my readers, friends, neighbors, community, state, and Nation to become one of the Awakened Ones. Do your own research from alternative, but reliable and truthful news sources (See Resources). Find out what you are eating, stop littering and buying plastic, stop smoking cigarettes and other nicotine products, plant a tree or shrub and stop cutting them down. Stop NOT caring about yourself, your children and your environment. Get educated and share with your tribe. Plant seeds of knowledge and wisdom. Together we can make a difference, but it takes one person at a time to make the change and begin planting seeds for good. So, will you play a role in the current worldwide shift? Or will you remain complacent?

We need to raise our consciousness to one of love. That may sound corny, but it means loving ourselves and our communities enough to create change. I love you. I love this little blue planet. Every single person is experiencing an energy flux. This means we are going through a change whether we want to or not. Now, we can each suffer through the changes or we can be wide awake and in flow.

To begin the process of being in flow we need to be mindful. Mindfulness is being in the present moment and giving our full attention to whatever we are doing to the complete exclusion of everything else. This is not to say we ignore the people and things around us. It means giving ourselves, whole and complete to the task before us.

When we are mindful in everything we become present, aware and awake. When we are aware and awake we see things more clearly, we understand more deeply. If we can see and understand more deeply and clearly we can know who we are authentically. Now, some people are just lost. Those are the people who appear to enjoy hurting others. You know those types. They're always causing trouble, stealing, hurting people, killing, lying, destroying property, etc. They appear lost and uncaring about life in general. In reality they are in deep and severe pain. So much pain that they need to make themselves feel better by hurting others. By hurting others they feel a sense of power and control, but that power is fleeting and not real power. Yes, mental illness comes in to play as well.

I once worked in a jail with both men, women and an ICE unit. We need to reform our prison systems even at the juvenile level of correction. What needs to happen is allowing these prisoners to know who they truly are. They need to hear that they are good people with skills, talents and gifts just like everyone else. They need to be taught to use their gifts in ways that will propel them into a higher consciousness.

Some people in the criminal justice system are so internally damaged they are unable to see any good in themselves. They believe they will never amount to anything, but why? Because that's what they've been told throughout their lives. It is the self-fulfilling prophecy at work. As well, many of the Correctional officers contribute to the trauma and devastation these inmates have endured. I am not against correctional officers, and I know their jobs are just as tough as police officer's jobs, but I do believe they could use some additional training on human rights, If you're told a lie over and over for your entire life, you can't help but believe it and then act on it.

You see, being mindful as it originates in ancient cultures is not only needed, it's necessary. We must become mindful in all we do. Wake up, Clear your eyes so you can see clearly. Get busy and start saving your own life so you can save the planet.

*"I will see you at the top. If you need a
hand that's what I'm here for.
To help you get there! I am your only hope. Believe in me.
Yours Truly, Truly, Truly, Ego!"*
Dr. Sandy Range

CHAPTER THREE

The Ego: Who Are You Anyway?

I am awesome! I'm cool baby. I am all you need to know. I am powerful beyond measure. I am your best friend. I have all the answers. I am your inspiration and your motivation. I am the one who will get you there. Believe me. I'm all you have! I'm all you need. I am superior. I am in control. I am Ego!

Ego wants us to believe that it is in control of everything we do and say. It does serve a purpose and is connected to the primitive part of our brain that rules fight, flight or freeze. It will protect itself at all cost by keeping us from walking out in front of a moving truck or jumping off a cliff. It wants us to survive. If we do not survive it will not survive as well and it loves being in the limelight.

Ego is protective, but also has a dark side, a controlling side. It will make you think you are the cat's meow! It will make you think you are self-important. It will make you think you know everything there is to know and no one can tell you any different. Ego is very smart and also manipulative. Very religious or spiritual people may believe they are filled with spirit, the Holy Ghost or whatever one may believe. The whole "speaking in tongues" thing is a farce. For those who claim they speak in tongues, they too, should know what they are saying and if there is no interpreter they should wait to be alone and speak directly to God (I Corinthians 14:27-28). In actuality, when a person truly speaks in tongues, everyone else who is graced with the Holy Spirit should understand them too!

Even very spiritual people who follow some of the mainstream practices like yoga, reiki, meditation, Buddhism, etc. can be caught up in an egocentric mind. If you have ever taken a class in one or more of these practices see if you can remember your teacher behaving as the know all – be all of the discipline. Did he or she present as self-important or place him/her self on a pedestal and ask for adoration. Did he or she really care about your spiritual learning or just the physical? Was the teacher angry or distressed while teaching? These questions and more should be asked of yourself while taking a class.

The ego allows one to believe they are endowed with the Holy Spirit or divine inspiration, then takes control so the person is quite different behind closed doors or anywhere outside of church, temple, synagogue, mosque or spiritual center.

I know you know some of these people. Could you be one of those people yourself (holy horrors!)? The hard part, right now, is to recognize and acknowledge that you are one of those people, if you are. Once you do, you can begin your transformation and put ego in check. If you desire true spirituality and to become your divinity you'll need a transformation, but ego will always be there to tempt you into thinking your thoughts are completely yours and not IT's!

Life has a way of moving us onto a new and sometimes very different path. At times that path may seem not to be chosen by us and something that we may never have chosen for ourselves. On a larger scale, our country is a perfect example. It appears split, divided and broken. Many of us feel broken or at least disillusioned, and can't see a way to peace for all.

Here is the lesson: What is happening in our country and the world is a reflection of humanity's collective ambivalence to and about our country and our planet. We've been ambivalent for a very long time.

There are those of us who focus on our individual needs, wants and desires to maintain what is best for ourselves no matter who it hurts in the process: the status quo. Selfish, individual needs are a primary importance and some will fight and even kill to maintain the status quo. Then there are those who fight against cruelty, discrimination, racism, sexism, misogyny, etc. and will fight to the death, literally. We are even labeled "far right extremists" and "leftist liberals." It makes no sense because, with the exception of a few individuals on both sides, everyone wants basically the same thing.

There are those who are connected to the earth, our families and societies and do what we can to create change, a shift in consciousness to the reality of the chaos that is happening now. If you are one of those people whose consciousness in elevated, even just a little; if you are one of those people who recognize there is something wrong; if you are one of those people who know without a doubt that change must happen, then it's time to take action. It's time to begin on a personal level and gather your internal, collective consciousness troops. Right and left move to the center then up collectively.

The set of "can dos" have to do with stepping out of our comfort zones and moving into a space of collective evolution. Here, we see the bigger picture, the global picture. If we are not looking at the whole picture we are still living in an ego controlled mindset. After all, if we are attempting to awaken ourselves on an individual basis and we are living to help ourselves improve and evolve, how can we say we are truly awakening if we are not inclusive of the entire planet? It is our home after all. When this planet is gone so are we.

Blessings heal, uplift, inspire, shift awareness, raise consciousness, and help all the world and its sentient beings become more intimate and compassionate. Wherever you are and whatever you are doing, at any given time, send a blessing. Bless yourself. You can't imagine what sending a blessings either out right or silently, can do for someone. Sending blessings is an energy exchange. You are sending out from you a gift that uplifts and heals. It also returns to you.

If you don't feel ready to step forward on your path of awakening, then just know that you are and will be guided by your ego. The densely mattered ego. Stuck in a perpetual pattern of mistrust, selfishness (Me, me, me. Mine, mine, mine) and spiritual dormancy. This is not the way to live. In this state of spiritual dormancy and stagnancy we never seem to find our happiness and peace of mind. We never see with better eyes. We never know what is coming down the road that will affect us. And we will never feel truly loved and will never truly love.

What most of us feel when we think we love someone, whether a romantic partner, family member, friend or whomever, is attachment. There are jealousies, mistrust, lies, infidelities and so much more that compels us into a state of unhappiness with the one we supposedly love. Love is free. Love is not binding or jealous. Ego causes us to end up feeling self-important and desire for our partner to serve our needs. If you perform an act of kindness for your loved one and he or she does not reciprocate, do you become angry, sad, depressed or some other unhappy emotional state. This is the controlling state of the ego lead mind.

How is one to understand why some people choose this blind lifestyle – unable to see, unable to love, unable to give or receive compassion? I suppose that no matter what frequency you are traveling this world at, we have all been there at some point in our lives. We have all been blind to love when it was real. We have all been mistrusting of others when we needed them most. We have all turned our backs on others when they needed us most. We have all been ego-lead jerks at one point. No, maybe we didn't know or realize that ego was guiding us, but then, there came a time when something shook us awake. We either tried to stay awake and continue to walk that path or we chose to go back to sleep because the awakening work was too much for us.

The Law of Cause and Effect

"What am I doing wrong?" It's a question many of us ask, throughout our lives, when we are really doing everything in our power to do the right things, follow the straight and narrow path and live with moral and ethical responsibility. Yet, there comes upon us some kind of devastation, a debilitation, a hindrance that won't let go. And so, we finally look up and ask this proverbial question.

It's almost inconceivable that through our blood, sweat and tears, ever nearing the end goal that we are forced off the chosen path, pushed beyond where we desire to go and left without knowing why. All of our hard work seems for naught and we must pick up the pieces and start again. But how often does one give up? We might say, "I just can't do this anymore!" We lose hope and faith in ourselves even though we know we have a power within that brought us this far.

We might assume we are not worthy or that we don't have what it takes or even that we are in some way bad! Whether this calamity is a loss of relationship, job/career, a business, a home or even a loved one to the next life, it's not about what we are doing wrong! It is about the Universal Law of Cause and Effect: Karma!

We need to take some time and look deeply at our spiritual paths and then ask the important questions: What am I supposed to learn from this this issue, problem, situation? What is the connection I need to make? In what ways does this thing help me to grow and evolve?

Karma is not a crazy, hippie thing from the 60's and 70's of the 20th century. Karma is the *law* of cause and effect, on the soul level, since the beginning of time. We are each a soul having an earthly existence in order to move forward in our evolution. By Divine design we are each created to join with a physical body and to align with this physical brain mind. We join with the brain mind in the womb and at birth we are shielded with a veil of forgetfulness of our true being. As young children we are more connected to our soul selves, but our upbringing and society gradually forces us into complete forgetfulness of who we truly are.

Karma is the lessons learned or missed in each of our lifetimes. We return again and again until we learn the lessons we are meant to for our evolution in spirit. It is not a punishment. It is a gift for those of us who will recognize our divinity as soul beings. YOU are soul. I AM soul. WE are soul. All of us together. And there is a way to reduce or eliminate negative karma as well!

So, it's not what we've done wrong. It's not about unworthiness or being bad! It's about what we chose to experience in this lifetime and to learn from it. Once all the lessons are learned we evolve beyond the confines of this earth density. We become ever evolving souls with new work in the spiritual realms. Work that is pleasing, surrounded by purely loving spirits and beauty. If we choose we can return in order to assist other souls on the path or continue to assist from the higher realms of Light.

The Source of All that Is, is the ultimate goal. The Ineffable One is all knowing and desires for His/Her creations to return to Him/Her. We are those creations, the Soul Beings sojourning on Earth to eventually return to our true home. The next calamity that comes along…or the current situation that is plaguing you, just remember your soul self and ask for the lesson to be learned!

Now, the nitty gritty on karma. Keep this page open! Karma really is the law of cause and effect on both a physical, and spiritual level, we, as humans, are pure spiritual beings driving around in this material, fleshy vehicle. Because we are tethered to this vehicle, ego (brain mind) was created to help protect it. When we decided to come to this earth plane we were still in the form of spirit. We went about our business happy and complacent. The longer we stayed and the more we became attached to this plane, the denser our physical bodies became. Walking and moving through this physical/material reality, we began to lose our identity with our true spiritual selves. Try to understand this physical reality as you are getting into your car. You start the ignition, step on the gas and drive to your destination. You then get out of your car and go about your business. Our bodies are our car, our vehicle used to drive us through this life until we reach our destination: spirit! This is also a good reason to maintain your body vehicle as you are unable to trade it in for a new one.

As well, we know we have been born into this earth plane many times attempting to learn the lessons we need to rejoin our brothers and sisters back home in the spiritual realms of being. Have you ever felt a déjà vu? Or felt you knew a place you've never been to before or a person you've never met before and had an instant connection with? Or maybe you feel like you never belonged here on this plane of existence? You've been here before, but from where did you come? Haha!

Why we repeat our lifetimes so many times, and sometimes thousands of times, is because we are not learning. We keep repeating the same mistakes lifetime after lifetime. It is karma that keeps tabs on us. Now, karma is not a being or an entity. Karma is a law of the universe. It's just the way it is.

Karma is the result of our thoughts, actions and behaviors in past lives and the current lifetime we are in: Cause and Effect. You think really nasty thoughts about someone because your ego feels that person has insulted you, hurt you, inflicted pain upon you, disagreed with you, said no to you etc. So, you become angry, hurt and begin thinking how much pain you could inflict upon that person in return. You want to get even and make him or her pay dearly for insulting your ego. Thoughts are energy. We are energy. Those nasty thoughts you're sending out, even though you may never act upon them, are affecting that person place or situation. Time has sped up (more on this later) and the results of the effects of our karma are coming back to us much more quickly. What goes out from you returns to you.

Our time on this earth has sped up and the results of our thoughts and actions are more readily being addressed nearly spontaneously. We are reaping what we have sown much more quickly and we're not understanding why we are always suffering. We continue to suffer, socially, financially, emotionally, mentally, and spiritually because we are still asleep. We sleepwalk through our lives never recognizing the bigger picture or plan for our true selves, the spirit self. When we begin to speak with kinder words, listen with softer ears, behave with more compassion we can then begin to awake to our true destinies.

There is more mental and physical illness now than ever before. We have become a society that experiences uninterrupted sickness. The negativity we keep in our thoughts can manifest in the body as illness and dis-ease over time. Hypertension, diabetes, heart failure, cancer. These are all manifestations of a mind gone bad or rancid. It doesn't help that we are poisoned each and every day by the toxic chemicals in our environment and our food.

We need to be mindful of our thoughts. Begin there. Pay attention to your every thought and what energy you are sending out into the world. When we voice our negative thoughts we are putting the power of the spoken word behind it intensifying the energy. "Before you speak let your words pass through three gates: is it true, is it necessary, is it kind" (Rumi).

We can also be aware of the tone of voice we use. Are we loud and boisterous? Are we breaking the sound barrier when we're upset? Or are we calm and soothing and a pleasure to listen to. There is a proverb by Gregory Y. Titleman: "you catch more flies with honey than vinegar." Are you soft and sweet or abrasive and acidic? You will be heard more readily when you speak in a soft calming voice than when you are screaming or yelling. Remember, it take two people to have an argument. When one person is simply quiet and listening or leaves the space, the other person has no one to argue with. This too, when we speak softly, even quieting our voice to a near whisper, the other person has to quiet down to hear what we are saying. It also calms the other person. Or if they persist, let them go it alone.

Karma is the result of our thoughts and behaviors. I cannot state this fact enough. We will continue to suffer, to be miserable, depressed, anxious and ill for as long as we continue on our current path. Self-importance or humility? That is the question and that is the roadmap to freedom. Humility does not mean being a doormat. Humility is a way of quieting the ego. It is ego that is the loud, abrasive, self-important one. As spirit in a human body we are naturally at peace with ourselves. We know who we are and therefore have no need to feel self-important. Being humble means respecting all of life in all of its various forms for who and what it is. When we respect life we respect ourselves and honor our true being and the trueness within others.

Now I know some of you are saying, yes, but how do I deal with someone who is out of control or a really awful boss, or a parent or spouse who is unbearably over powering? This is how karma works: We have each chosen, before our births, to what family, society, and culture we would be born into. In doing so, from the higher realms, we chose this life in order to evolve through the lessons it would teach us. Some of us choose very difficult lives in order to evolve more quickly, but only if we are able to recognize the lessons and learn from them. The trauma of birth (and veil of forgetfulness) causes us to forget our life before this life.

The following is extremely important for parents and caregivers of very young children. As I stated in chapter one, when children begin to explore life even within a few months of birth, they tend to see things we don't see as adults. As toddlers and new speakers, children may develop invisible friends with whom they play and talk. Young children are also very imaginative and creative. They create visual worlds where everything is happy and playful. As they get a little older, maybe 5 years old, the imagination becomes powerful. What is happening is that very young children are still connected to the spirit realm. Without parental or caregiver intervention these children may be able to stay connected to their true selves, their spirit selves and evolve in this life more quickly, even eliminating karmic influences of a past life or lives.

It is the parents, teachers, and other authority figures in the child's life who destroy any connection to the spirit realms the child might have. We, as parents and thinking we are doing what is best for our child, begin telling these children to STOP imagining things, STOP being so silly or playful, STOP talking to no one and on and on. That is our big mistake as caregivers. We destroy that connection instead of nurturing it. Better yet, as parents, when we recognize these imaginings and creativity in our children we should go with it. Nurture it, Talk to our children. Ask them what they see or are doing and with whom. Allow then to draw pictures of what they see and ask them to explain (if they can). Remember, in terms of spirit, they may know and identify with the spirit realm internally, but may not have the language to describe it. It is also a good idea to teach your child/ren that they should only express their spiritual insights at home with you or with others who understand and are nurturing and compassionate. Not everyone in mainstream society is ready for children, even adults, with this knowledge and connection to spirit.

It is not your fault! You are also a victim of your upbringing. Your parent raised you according to how they were parented, as are their parents and the parents before them. Our society tells us to behave a certain way to maintain control over us. All world societies have done the same thing with the exception of only a few cultures. Today, we are seeing more inner work being done and more raising of consciousness in the world. We don't hear about that very much because mainstream media focuses on the negative in the world. However, there is a very big movement happening behind the scenes all over the world. People are recognizing their true selves and attempting to follow a path to raise their consciousness to a state of divinity.

We can see this in countries that are refusing polluted and genetically engineered or modified crop seeds; we see nations where the people are standing up against the cruelties of their governments. We see people performing tasks and creating ideas and products that help minimize waste and pollution. We see people fighting for human rights, animal rights, plant rights (our rainforests, etc.) It's not in the news every day, but it is happening on a grand scale. We still have a lot of work to do in the United States. I know within myself that we will be redeemed and put on the path of enlightenment as a country. It is up to each one of us individually to make this happen collectively. You are important in this process and that is what this book is about. We need to stop allowing our government to hold us captive in this slavery of the mind. We seem to swallow whatever they dish out even if it's bad for us.

Ego sits at the head of the table right now in all governments. During one of my meditation classes I was asked about our current president. My response was this: "I believe he became the president to wake us all up. He is exposing what has been happening behind closed doors. He is so perpetually undermining our rights, our health, our wellbeing as citizens we have no choice but to see the truth." However, there are still those who are asleep and do not even vaguely understand the damage being done, even to them. However, I believe that this leader is a victim of his parenting and the ego driven need for power and control he was brought up with.

So, be mindful of your thoughts and behaviors. Even making judgements about others should be avoided. We are each on our own individual paths and some may not be as far along as you or me. We need to be able to let everyone be who they are at this point in time. When you look into someone's eyes know that they too are a child of the All That Is, just like us. Even those we might consider to be on a downward spiral or performing acts of violence or who lie and cheat and steal. These people are still children of the ALL, albeit, on a much lower frequency that we may be. The most we should do is send a blessings or plant a seed of wisdom for those we know or who are close to us. However, be mindful that you should never force your ideas onto someone else if they are not ready. You have planted the seed and now it is up to the person to nurture it and help it grow.

We can release karma from the past by how we are living in the present. Be mindful of everything you say and do and more importantly, your thoughts. The process is quite simple, but I never said it was easy. You and your true self are worth every bit of the growing pains you will experience on this path. You beautiful soul are valuable and uniquely special. Know this and act accordingly!

So many people are suffering in this world of ours. What can we do about it? How can we change the status quo? You might feel as though there is nothing you can do to make a difference; that you don't have the power to make change. And if you did do something it wouldn't matter because too many people just don't care! Well, you're right, at least partially.

People do care. They care about their own well-being. They care about their own happiness and making sure their needs are met. They care about how they look and what they wear. They care about what people think of them. They care about self! Me, me me…how selfish is that??? However, that is how we are raised. That is what happens when society dictates how we should be in this world. This is about the values and ethics we were taught to uphold.

Every one of us has the power to make change. We think "I'm only one person. What can I do to change things?" The way to make change in the world is to begin locally…very locally! Change begins with the self. Everyone strives to meet their own personal needs, but what if we expanded that just a little. What if, when you look in the mirror each morning you took an inventory of yourself: your attitudes, your thinking, your understanding, your tolerance, your acceptance, your compassion, your strengths and weaknesses, your willingness to change yourself for the better?

What if, every day, you smiled at any person you see when you leave the house? Could you say "Hello! You look great today!" to a stranger or a colleague, co-worker, associate, grocery store clerk? How do you think that person would respond? Sure, maybe they would give you the look (Is she/he crazy? I don't know you!), but they would walk away feeling great. They received a compliment that maybe they never receive from anyone. Maybe the walls of protection would being to crack and break down. Maybe, you just brightened his or her whole day!

We are all connected. Everything we say and do affects everyone else in significant and subtle ways. When you look in the mirror take that inventory. Make the necessary changes within in order to become a more highly evolved and enlightened person in all ways: physically, mentally, emotionally, and spiritually. Once we begin to change ourselves the people around us notice. We become role models and mentors for evolved thinking and behavior.

This does not mean to become complacent with your safety and security, but it does mean acceptance. Realize that no one on our beautiful blue planet wants to suffer and everyone desires happiness. When we learn to be in acceptance of others, accepting the level of evolution they are currently in and understanding that they are growing (however slowly or rapidly), we then understand that we are all on the same path. Once we are on the path to enlightened being, we change the world one person at a time. Remember, there are already hundreds of thousands of people around the world and right here in the USA who are doing this work.

Think about the changes you can make within yourself to assist in your own growth and evolution. The joy of enlightened thinking and being is incredible. You don't have to be a monk, a nun, a priest or rabbi. All you need is to make the choice to become better and help humanity along the way. Each of us counts. Not one of us should be left behind. Imagine being an enlightened soul, emanating your inner light. You are so full of joy and you navigate life fearlessly. People are drawn to your light and seek the knowledge to become the same. Would you not share your transformation to help them along the path? Of course you would. And of course, ego would not!

Now, just one more important point about ego and karma. A very important point and one that may insult ego itself! The Mind! ...Arrggh! Our cognitive functioning has to do with our perceptions, how we learn, process information and gain knowledge. Sometimes, we short circuit a lot or just a little resulting in poor insight, poor judgement & decision making, confusion, altered perception, racing thoughts, worry, not finding the right words, poor memory, forgetfulness and so much more.

As well, cognitive problems can bring on a host of physical problems: insomnia, body aches and pains, headaches, stomach problems, lethargy, and if left alone too long emotional trauma can eat away at you in the form of cancer. "When emotional trauma goes unhealed, the body system is in a constant state of heightened stress. Numerous studies have connected stress with lower immune function and higher incidences of disease in general. A recent report, however, analyzed the findings of close to a hundred other studies that showed how the sympathetic nervous system (SNS) can actually encourage metastasis when it is chronically activated." (How Emotional Trauma Can Create Cancer. Dr. Veronique Desaulniers).

Knowing when it happens and recognizing these decreased areas of cognitive functioning is a start to improving our overall health. Many people, when we realize that we may be short circuiting in a couple of areas, become embarrassed or attempt to hide and camouflage these issues. What happens? It gets worse over time.

With the exception of Alzheimer's disease, Autism Spectrum Disorders, Traumatic Brain Injuries or other neurological disorders, finding the right counselor or therapist can help restore healthy functioning without medication! Holistic therapists address the whole of you and not just the symptoms of a problem. A holistic therapist will help you get to the root cause of your issues and begin working from there.

There are many methods and techniques that can be used to help bring cognitive dysfunction to a healthy normative functioning. The key is to know when you need help. If you have only an occasional bout of forgetfulness (misplaced keys for instance), not to worry. However, if you forget where you placed your keys more often than not you may need to seek outside help.

Some of the methods used by holistic therapists include: mindfulness, meditation, tapping, yoga, hypnotherapy, reiki, sound therapy, energy healing and a host of other techniques. Many of these methods have proven to restore balance and harmony in the mind and body, however, they are usually not covered by insurance. Along with holistic counseling, where insurance may be accepted, these methods allow for healing in a non-invasive, non-threatening way, and leave you with a sense of peace, calm, balance, grounding and strength.

So, if you find yourself experiencing any of the above symptoms of the mind, seek help early! Don't wait too long! All licensed therapists must abide by confidentiality rules and a code of ethics.

*"When we realize that we are children
of the Source of all creation,
we can understand our place in it and
our unique reasons for Being."*
Dr. Sandy Range

CHAPTER FOUR

Higher Intelligence – Divine mind

The mind is not just housed in the brain and the brain is more than just an organ that keeps the body functioning on auto pilot. For the purpose of this book I will focus on the mind and its power of thought processes.

There has been a great deal of debate around this concept. The mind, however, can also be thought of as an aspect of the soul, in the sense of being both mind and soul being divine and immortal. It links human thinking with the infinite principle of the Universe.

There is a duality to the mind in the form of your conscious mind and your subconscious mind. The conscious mind is that part of your thinking processes that deal with the present and recent past, as well as the immediate future. It is that part of you that deals with what is in its present form. Have you ever been on information overload? Your conscious mind seems to tune out or even shut down when overwhelmed with too much information too often. That's ok. It's a very useful process.

Your subconscious mind is that part of you that serves as your storehouse of information: memories, experiences, learning and programming throughout your lifetime. It is also the part of you through which your conscious mind reacts and responds to the present according to its programming. Think of the conscious and subconscious mind as an iceberg. The twenty percent above water is your conscious mind. The eighty percent below water is your subconscious mind.

But wait, there is another aspect of the mind. The superconscious mind. Ask yourself this question and before you answer, think deeply about your answer:

Who is the thinker of your thoughts?

If you really consider this question, you will realize that there is something greater within you. Something divine and immortal. A person does not say, "arm hurts." You say "*my* arm hurts." The person denotes possession of one's arm: "my arm." The person is not the arm itself: "arm hurts." There is a greater, higher consciousness at work within a human being that knows it is the possessor of its body and not the body itself. Not even the brain. There is a much higher force and intelligence at work within us. That part of us that is the possessor of our bodies is Soul, our Spiritual intelligence and life force.

The superconscious mind is that part of you that is connected to a higher source, an infinite intelligence. It is where your inspiration, ideas, imagination, creativity and knowing come from. It is that part of you connected to the All That Is. It is your muse, your motivation, your inspiration and your source of imagination and vision.

All thought comes from the mind: the conscious, subconscious and superconscious mind. Thought is simply energy as are our bodies and everything in existence. As far as thought is concerned each time you think a thought it goes out from you in the form of vibrational energy. It is an electromagnetic energy in that it will attract a like vibrational energy to it. Like attracts like, the law of Cause and Effect and the Law of Attraction.

If you think about the way the Universe works, everything, and I mean everything, is in a circle or cycle. The planets rotate around the sun. The seasons of the earth rotate equally through winter, spring, summer and fall. Even the human life in physical form is cyclic from birth, infancy, adolescence, adulthood, old age and then death, then a new life is born and the cycle repeats again. The electromagnetic energy of our thoughts is cyclic as well. Your thoughts are released from your mind into the world and universe in the form of energy. They gather similar vibrational energies and that energy, quickened and amplified, eventually returns to you in varied forms. We really do create our own realities by the thoughts we think. What you think about you bring about!

Susan Pockett in the "Nature of Consciousness" writes: The Electromagnetic field of the mind [brain] comprises a universal consciousness that experiences the sensations, perceptions, thoughts and emotions of every conscious being in the universe.," Professor John Joe McFadden from the School of Biomedical and Life Sciences at the University of Surrey (UK) reports, "Scientists can find no region or structure in the brain that specializes in conscious thinking. Consciousness remains a mystery. Consciousness is what makes us 'human." Professor McFadden continues saying, "Language, creativity, emotions, spirituality, logical deduction, mental arithmetic, our sense of fairness, truth, ethics, are all inconceivable without consciousness."

This is very important because we must, at all cost, be very careful of what we are thinking. "What we think about, we bring about." If your thoughts are of a low vibrational energy (negative or dense energy), that is what you will bring into your immediate world. It is what you attract back to yourself, again, cause and effect. If you think you will never achieve greatness, you never will because that is the thought energy you are focused on.

Now, if you are constantly in a consciousness of negativity about money, abundance or prosperity, or even about love, relationships, business or your social life you are in a consciousness of perpetual lack. This means your thoughts are in a very low vibrational energy. In order to raise that vibration of energy you need to reprogram your subconscious mind, the storehouse. This is where reprogramming of faulty thinking comes in.

The Subconscious Mind has a Story

In the storehouse of the subconscious lies all of the experiences, learning and programming we have received throughout our entire lives. It is the cause of the conscious mind's reactions and responses to stimuli in the present. Remember we said that the subconscious mind is the eighty percent of the iceberg lying below the water level? That eighty percent is one massive storehouse! It is the fuel that powers the conscious mind. What is stored in the subconscious is the result of our learning, programming and conditioning from birth.

Much of how we respond to our everyday existence is because of the conditioning and programming we received in early childhood. We come into the world free souls, unblemished, pure and honest. We are wide open, innocent and eager to learn, grow and evolve. And no, there is no *Original Sin*. For many of us that early conditioning, be it from the positive or negative experiences and modeling from our caregivers, is what drives us today. It becomes how we react and respond to the world.

So imagine that your parent or caregiver experienced a traumatic event that was never treated or healed. The hypervigilance, lack of sleep, anxiety, fear, anger and other dysfunctional coping mechanisms that the caregiver presents with are models for the young child's (in his or her care) behaviors and reactions to every day events and circumstances. The child grows up thinking it is normal that 'I should be fearful/anxious of everything.'

Or maybe the child is a victim of abuse or neglect. Even verbal abuse, as we know, can cause severe damage to the psyche of a child and last through adulthood. "You're no good. You'll never amount to anything. Who do you think you are? You're stupid. You're a knucklehead. You're a waste. I wish you were never born…" I could go on and on, but I'm sure you get the point.

A fragile child will carry these verbal daggers deep within believing the story he or she has been told over and over again. It is the proverbial "self-fulfilling prophecy." It can even lead to suicide. We don't want that. Not to mention physical abuse and sexual assault. These can leave mental, emotional and physical scars that last a lifetime if they are not addressed and healed.

It is also with those who are always feeling depressed, sad, anxious or angry. Most people do not realize that it is your thoughts that create those feelings. "What you think about you bring about." So now we have an idea of how the conscious and subconscious minds work to our favor or our defeat.

So here you are. Here I am. Who are we really? In order to answer that question I need to explain that our material, physical world is an illusion termed Maya in Sanskrit (Hinduism). Many ancient cultures around the world are very aware of this illusory state. It is in the West that we are still sleep walking through this illusory world.

We see many spiritual leaders, as well as, regular folks who practice true meditation that go into a trance state where one can receive information and communicate with spirit beings. Medicine people, Shamans, Healers, Holy Men & Women truly devout ministers, priests and monks all go into the spirit realm to receive information on how to heal someone or provide help for self or others, and they are connected to their collective societies. They become the community's healer.

We, in the West see this as the person going into an imaginary state of consciousness where the brain imagines other-worldly beings or perceived spiritual information. This state of consciousness might also cause the person experiencing this altered state of consciousness to be sent to a mental hospital and pumped full of *psychotropic* drugs (go figure) to keep the person asleep (figuratively speaking). The truth is that this physical world is the trance state and the spiritual world is the reality.

We are born spirit into this imaginary world of hardship to help us grow and evolve. It is classroom earth. We have become separate and apart from ourselves and our true being as spirit. The Vedic scriptures, an ancient Indian text, speak of Maya. Speaking on the Vedic scriptures, Paramahansa Yogananda wrote in his book, *The Autobiography of a Yogi*,"

> ...the physical world operates under one fundamental law of *maya*, the principle of relativity and duality. Since God in his absolute form is Complete Unity, the only way He can appear as the separate and diverse manifestations of creation is under a false or unreal veil of *maya*, or illusion.

So, is it God that created this classroom earth? No, we did, but we are sparks of God. This earth plane was created by us for the lessons that we need to learn, but it was an unconscious creation. As pure souls, the more we relished in the experiences of matter the denser we and it became. We soon forgot who we were and became what we are. It is illusory, but we perceive it as real, dense, heavy, physically overbearing, as we grew these vehicles we call a body.

However, God, in order to experience life, placed him/her self in every iota of the creation. Why did I say 'him/her self?' God is not a person, but contains within it every energy of our human life both male and female. God is the original intelligence of the Universe. It perceived itself into Being and expressed the desire to know itself even more and therefore began its creation to know itself more fully.

Yogananda also mentioned duality. In most esoteric spiritual practices or faiths, duality is recognized as the dream state of existence, the duality of separateness. This means we *perceive our existence as separate from our Source*. That whatever is perceived is duality in the form of separateness of mind and body. One is being the perceiver of a thought and not the thought or thing itself. This is illusion. What is more important is non-duality. Everything is One. We are not separate from everything in existence. We are part of everything in existence and it is part of us. So, how can we be so violent against one another, against ourselves, against nature, against life itself? When we hurt another we are hurting ourselves.

How do we get back to a state of oneness? By connecting to our higher intelligence; that of the Divine mind. Higher intelligence is beyond the rational thinking mind. It is beyond the emotional contributions to our thoughts. It is an intelligence that supersedes the physical, emotional and mental traps of duality. Higher Intelligence is connected to spirit. It allows us to see beyond the physical or known reality and receive information that solves the most difficult problems. Many people use their higher intelligence to create magnificent works of art, technology, science and, of course, spirituality. These people are the creators of new and unique ways to help us live in this world.

The superconscious mind or higher intelligence is even more than that. It is the cornerstone, the foundation of moving back (an oxymoron) to who we really are. It is the mind of our soul, but it is not Divine mind. Before we can discuss Divine mind we should first understand how to access our higher intelligence.

Mindfulness is one way to connect to higher mind. Being mindful of every thought, behavior, speech and actions will help us to connect with higher mind. When we are mindful we can acknowledge the thoughts we are having that are not helpful and in fact hurtful. We can pay more attention to what behaviors we're exhibiting that are either helpful or hurtful. Remember karma? Good! Then if we are acting accordingly we connect with higher mind more easily. One cannot express behaviors or thoughts that are harmful and expect that higher mind will be available. Only ego is available and taking the lead with negative thoughts and behaviors.

I cannot stress enough to practice mindfulness on a daily basis, even while you are sitting at home by yourself. It is important to understand your thought patterns and why you suddenly shift your thoughts to the negative. With mindfulness you become aware of when you are thinking poor thoughts and can stop them in their tracks, ask for forgiveness and let them go. The more we are mindfully aware of our own thoughts the more we shift into thought patterns that are healthy and filled with unconditional love. Suddenly we are living within a higher consciousness.

Once we reach that higher state of consciousness and are walking our talk, we can work toward Divine mind. Divine mind is always being divinely guided in everything we do. Divine mind allows us the opportunity to reach an even higher state of being, even while here on earth. As we are all a part of the whole of consciousness we connect, once again, to Infinite Intelligence or Universal Mind. This infinite intelligence is the mind that created it all. It is God Consciousness or Divine mind.

Wouldn't it be great to be able to move through the world always in a perpetual state of God consciousness? What would that mean? It means you have finally arrived. It means you have merged your soul self to the Source of Creation. It means your thoughts and behaviors are always in alignment with the All That Is. It means you are connected to Infinite intelligence. It means you are a light in the world. It means you retain peace always. It means you are becoming part of a global movement of higher minded, divinely intelligent beings on earth. It means you are no longer caught in the duality trap of ego existence as you once were. It means that you will be part of a global emergence of super minded beings. It means you are now a teacher and a guide to others seeking this path. Yes, you are!

Here is where the superconscious mind comes in to play. The Superconscious is the Universe. It is that part of you connected to the Divine. Your immortal self who is the eternal soul self and is connected to God and the Universe. Scientists have called this the unified field. Because we are made up of the components of the unified field we are one with the universe. Better yet, we are the universe.

*"When we realize that we are children
of the Source of all creation,
we can understand our place in it and our
unique and beautiful reasons for Being."*
Dr. Sandy Range

CHAPTER FIVE

The Bible or Fake News?

In the following two chapters I have written about the Christian Bible. That is because it was never complete and it bears some false witness. I wanted to provide some insights into one of the largest religions on this planet with this one book, the Bible, as its policy and procedure manual. Remember, be open to receive and you may gain some wisdom and insight of your own. The information for these two chapters came from a lot of research from scholarly texts, journals and books used to write my Doctoral Dissertation, so it does hold some weight! I do hope you are open to learning something fascinating as I was! Here goes:

What happened to us and why don't we know we are these divine beings? Well, the explanation may stop some of you in your tracks and that's okay. Just keep moving forward anyway! God, being Infinite Intelligence, made the creation, made the spirits we call angels or luminaries, made both lower and higher beings, made us (we are lower beings while on earth), but not the way most of us believe. In chapter one I spoke about God's manifestation of Self in order to know him/herself more fully and experience the creation itself. We were created as living beings, but we were not the first!

When the books of the bible were written by men who lived more than 2000 to 5000 years ago, and when they were found and placed in one single document or book we need to remember that the new single book did not contain all of the books written and neither was it written out verbatim. The book was edited for content and for control. It was a 19 year old Bishop named Irenaeus who dogmatically controlled the content of the new book called the bible. The following is a necessity in order for human souls to find *meaning making* in our divinity, but in a new and different way of understanding.

If we do not understand our creation we cannot understand our divinity.

What comes next will definitely throw some of you for a loop. However, I strongly advise you to read on and with an open mind. Open minds learn and grow and evolve. Closed minds will stay just as they are, stuck, stagnant and immovable. This equals no growth, no evolution, and no divinity. Now, it doesn't matter what faith or religion you are. What matters is that you understand where you came from and why you are here on this beautiful blue planet.

There is a lot of research in this chapter and you, the reader, are advised to do some research of your own. You can find the citations at the end of this book. So please bear with me over these next two chapters and you will learn something new about the Bible.

There have been many teachers of spiritual wisdom over the centuries. From Lao Tzu, to Buddha, from Yeshua or Jesus to the modern day prophet Edgar Cayce, and many, many more. In these current times, self-identified masters of spiritual wisdom still teach their flocks. In considering these spiritual teachings and Christian spiritual philosophies, this chapter's intent is to compare and reveal the metaphysical and esoteric teachings and wisdoms of the human condition as related to the understanding of the historical teachings of Christianity even prior to the appearance of the Christ Yeshua, but more so, during His time on this earth and after His resurrection.

The questions arise: What is the truth according to those who wrote down and/or orally passed on Spiritual teachings to human kind? Are there contradictions? Are there similarities? Did the early church fathers give us the whole truth? We already know there were massive book burnings to justify what they considered heresy. Was what they destroyed really heresy or is what they taught in the early Christian church heresy in itself considering their massive burnings of sacred texts and the senseless deaths and victimization of Gnostic Christians? Why were the Gnostics considered heretics? Why was Yeshua excluded from being a Gnostic according to early Christianity? Keep reading. He was a Gnostic!

What is the current ideology of the ancient teachings of Christianity? With the latest discoveries of ancient Gnostic texts such as the *Nag Hammadi Scriptures*, the *Dead Sea Scrolls* to name a few, what mysteries are revealed to us about our origins and our salvation? The answers, hopefully, will find common ground among the teachings humans have received over the centuries.

Every cultural, religious or spiritual/esoteric knowledge possesses some mythology. The words written down by men, after the teachings of the Master were provided, and sometimes centuries afterwards, may not be entirely accurate, may be embellished or missing vital information. Furthermore, we must consider the changes and omissions of Christianity's true teachings, purposefully executed, by the early priests and bishops establishing the first Christian church.

Hypothetically, we may find a more accurate truth or at least a more detailed explanation in the ancient texts and teachings that will bring us to a common truth about our Divinity and the teachings of Christ. In finding that truth humankind may indeed know One truth, or at least the right truth for one's self.

It is not the intent of this chapter to prove or disprove any particular religious belief, but to examine the history and philosophy of the Spiritual teachings and wisdoms of the ancient brotherhoods leading to and about Christianity, since in the west, Christianity is the mainstream religion or belief system. This chapter will attempt to provide a view on the historical teachings of the Christ, a new understanding of who we really are and our mission while on this earth according to the Gnostic Yeshua or Jesus.

We may never really know the whole truth of our existence and our divinity until we actually and individually transcend to that state of being. However, there are echoes of the original teachings passed on from the great Masters. If we look at the historical teachings of the secret brotherhoods of antiquity we may indeed find the original messages meant for our salvation, evolution of the soul and return to spirit.

In order to understand the revelations of why and how Jesus, Yeshua or Issa as he is sometimes called, came to the earth we must first compare two stories of creation: Christian Orthodox and Gnostic. Let us first look at the Bible's Old Testament view of Creation. "In the beginning God created the heaven and the earth." God created light and divided it from darkness. He divided the firmament from the waters which He called heaven (1:6-8). Under the waters He made the earth appear. He made the sun, the moon and the stars and all the animals and plants on the earth. One note: Genesis 1:25 states, "And God made the beast of the earth after His kind. . .and every thing that creepeth upon the earth after his kind." If this God would create beasts after His kind. His kind must also be beastly and creepy. Yes, He also created humankind: "Let us make man in our image, after our likeness. . .." Who are the "our" this passage speaks of and of what "kind" are they? We must ask the question, if God is unbegotten, ineffable and has no one above, below, before or after Him; If God is immeasurable without beginning or end, what gods or beings made humans, and the beasts of the earth in their own likeness?

Further, we can question nearly everything in the Book of Genesis, particularly Adam and Eve and their offspring. Genesis states Adam and Eve bore two sons, yet they were to go forth and multiply and fill the earth with their seed. It does not tell us how this happened with two males as offspring and one who was murdered by the other. We are not provided an explanation for this miraculous flourishing of human life and marriage to other women with whom Adam's offspring bore more children. Who were these other humans and where did they come from?

In the Christian Gnostic tradition, the God that we all praise according to the biblical scriptures is not the God that is the All that Is, the One true God, the Ineffable. The Nag Hammadi Scriptures state, "The One is a sovereign that has nothing over it. It is God and Parent Father of the All, the invisible one that is over the All that is incomprehensible, that is pure light at which no eye can gaze" The biblical god, according to Christian Gnosticism, is the creator god of heaven, earth and humankind. It is a god or archon that is inferior, filled with ignorance and was brought forth from a mistake, yet still part of the Ineffable's plan.

What the Orthodox Bible does not include in the creation story is the existence of the Mother, Barbelo, with her own aeon as the first emanation (Nag Hammadi). She is also called "Protennoia, the Divine First Thought." She was the first emanation of the Ineffable All that Is. It was from her, being the female aspect of the Great Father, the Ineffable, that the Ineffable Begotten Son, the Christ, came into being.

Let us start from the very beginning in order to understand the system that came forth from the Ineffable One, from beholding Himself and reflecting on His image, to the creation of the aeons, the orders, powers and Yaldabaoth, the son of Sophia (wisdom), Creator of the world. "He [the Ineffable] reflects on His image everywhere. Sees it in . . . the Spirit, becomes enamored in the luminous water. . . surrounding Him. . . His thought became reality, and *she* who appeared in His presence in shining light came forth." According to the *Secret Book of John* (Nag Hammadi), 'she' is Barbelo or Protennoia, the First Power, the Divine Mother. "She is the first thought, the image of the [Ineffable] spirit. She became the universal womb, for she precedes everything."

In antiquity women were regarded as inferior in both the Orthodox and Gnostic scriptures and not much has changed today. However, we see that the female spirit was the first pure spirit brought forth from the Ineffable. She was the Mother of all creation above and below. Without her there would be no heavenly realms, no benevolent and divine beings, no humans and no Christ. However, we must remember to view these beings (in the immortal realms) as pure spirit, without a body, without gender, and made of pure energy or light. We must not mistake seeing them as we see ourselves as humans. They are something else, emanations of the Ineffable One, but were named human: our predecessors.

As well, the feminine or Mother spirit is kept out of Orthodox Christianity. According to the Church there is no Mother, Son and Holy Spirit as One emanation of the Ineffable, what we call the Father or God. And when we began to include the Mother, as in Father-Mother God, people were labeled new agers, cultists or just crazy (heretical).

Out of the union of the Ineffable Spirit and the Divine Mother Barbelo, the first power and first aeon, came the emanation of the Ineffable Himself "the self-generated child" (Nag Hammadi) in perfection and "everything was established by the will of the Holy Spirit through the Self Generated... This was the only Child of the Father-Mother that had come forth... the pure light." This child is the Anointed One, the Christ. The Holy Spirit is the tether and breath of the Ineffable unbegotten One to all that came forth out of Him. It is our connection, no matter how fleeting or fragile or seemingly non-existent, to the Divine and our true home.

It is from these first emanations or reflections of the All that Is that the first divine and pure emanations came into being. We must keep in mind that the names that are given to these emanations represent a virtue or quality of their being. We don't know if humans provided these names or if the names were taught to humans from visitations from the upper realms. Remember the prophets, the channels who received information from Divine Beings, just as there are channels or prophets today who receive Divine information from the ascended masters. It is shameful that most people today do not regard these prophecies and knowledge as real.

Though considered androgynous, having the qualities of both male and female energy, other divine beings came into existence from mind given as a companion by the Holy Spirit to the self-generated one, the Christ. They were made in pairs of male and female (energy) able to produce and bring forth their own realms with kingdoms of light in a hierarchy consequent of the immeasurable aeons.

In the Pistis Sophia we are told that as the aeons/realms were created from highest to lowest (see Sequence of Aeons. Gnostic Church of L.V.X, appendix i), and three being that of the Ineffable realms (the highest) excluding the Ineffable unbegotten region (Pistis Sophia), the creation of beings that came forth into the lowest twelve aeons became more and more distorted and mutated. These are the beings of the lower realms from the emanation of Yaldabaoth the son (creation) of Sophia or the emanation of wisdom.

Now, Sophia originally dwelled in the thirteenth aeon of the emanation of the Ineffable. The aeons were created as such that anyone dwelling in any particular aeon could not see past the veil of the aeon above the one in which one dwelled. Because of her faith and her love for the Ineffable, Sophia was given permission of the Ineffable to look upward past the veils into the upper aeons and into the heights of the "Treasury of Light." She longed to ascend to that region out of devotion and ultimate love for the Ineffable One. In doing so she neglected to perform the Mystical duties of her own realm. While performing this devotion she endured the wrath of those in her own realm and those of the twelve realms below her. We shall understand how some of those in realms furthest away from the treasury of Light showed to be unsound or fallible.

Sophia's mate, the third triple power (self-willed) of the thirteenth aeon did not comply with his order and purpose. He never shared the completeness of his light and purification with his partner as did the other rulers of the higher aeons. He, instead, had a desire to gain control and mastery over all of the thirteenth aeon, and therefore Sophia lacked in the completeness of her Light. Jealous of Sophia's longing to ascend above them all, Self-willed joined forces with the powers of the twelfth aeon below and created a great emanation, that of a beast with a lion's head, and a hoard of other beastly emanations in that lower realm. He sought to trick Sophia and have his creations devour her Light in order to destroy her (Pistis Sophia).

A light, similarly as brilliant as that of the Treasury of Light, emanated from below in the twelfth aeon which is only shadow and darkness (the chaos). The third triple power had given a portion of his light to the beastly emanation he created and it shone up into the thirteenth aeon attracting Sophia. Through her longing to ascend to that great height above she saw this light below her and assumed it was a light like that of the Treasury of Light. Sophia had the good intention of going into that aeon below and taking that light to create a beautiful aeon with a kingdom and beings like those above.

As Sophia stood over the chaotic matter without spirit within it, she became distressed at what she saw. What emanated from her desire to make things right was also disturbing. The lion faced entity came to her and was frightful to her. Her wish was to change the ugliness of that being and that realm. Sophia blew her light into the entity's face with the desire of making this being like one of the divine beings above to "rule over matter and all its powers" (Pistis Sophia).

This was the first Archon of the abyss. Although androgynous it came forth with a strong power of its own. However, this archon had no idea who created it or that there were any aeons above it being unable to see through the veils above its own realm. It was ignorant of the Ineffable One and its emanations of Light. It only knew of its mother-creator, Sophia, who blew her light into it.

Yaldabaoth was the result of Sophia's innocent attempt to create a realm and more beings like herself, filled with the Light of the Ineffable One, but without her partner's fullness and without consent of the Holy Spirit. The result of this creation was Yaldabaoth who Sophia hid from all in the higher realms by casting it away from her to an even lower realm. Only the Holy Spirit knew of this being. Yaldabaoth, the first ruler or archon, moved far from his place of origin. (Nag Hammadi).

Sophia's fall was great. Yaldabaoth then created his own realms having inherited the great creative light-power of his mother Sophia. The emanation below became envious of her Light that was greater than his, but not full and complete. He created more chaos out of which wrath came into existence in all the realms below it, and water and matter came into manifest being, but was cast out. (Nag Hammadi).

Yaldabaoth, created seven aeons of heaven, each with its own ruler. He also created five more rulers to "reign over the depths of the abyss" (116) or the underworld, twelve aeons in all. Yaldabaoth was misinformed and ignorant of the immortal beings in the aeons above him. He thought of himself the only god. He spoke to his creations saying, "I am god and there is no other god beside me." And furthermore, that he was "a jealous god" (Nag Hammadi), (Bible: Exodus).

Yaldabaoth creates seven heavens, however, these heavens are shielded from the immortal and perfect aeons above him where the pure beings of Light from the Ineffable reside. He is unaware of the Light aeons above him. He is only able to know of his mother (creator), Sophia (wisdom) who repented and was forgiven after a long penance, but placed in a realm directly above that of Yaldabaoth. It is because of his ignorance and the power and light he took from her, that Yaldabaoth assumed he was an immortal god with no others beside himself.

Now, we might think that Yaldabaoth is the devil. He is not. If we look back we'll remember the permission Sophia was given to look through the veils of the aeons above her, into the Treasury of Light, then we can understand there was a design to the creation of the realms below. As well, we can see how each immortal aeon, beginning with the first, the Barbelo aeon, created other immortal aeons through the power and light of the Ineffable One. These designed lower aeons gave way to human beings, us, that were initially imperfect.

The bible speaks of the creation of the first humans, Adam and Eve. God then created Adam from the earth and created Eve from Adam's rib. Their residence was the Garden of Eden, a paradise where they were given free reign over the land, plants and the animals:

> Then God said, "Let us make mankind in our image, after our likeness, and let them have dominion over the fish of the sea and the fowl of the air, and over the cattle and over all the earth, and over every creeping thing that creepeth upon the earth. So God created man in his own image, in the image of God created he him; male and female created he them (Genesis.1:26, 27).

The Book of Genesis further reports this god had "breathed into [Adam's] nostrils and he became a living soul." According to the Secret Book of John, Yaldabaoth hears a voice from the realms above him saying, "Humanity exists… and the Child of Humanity" (Nag Hammadi). However, Yaldabaoth didn't understand where the voice came from and thought that it came from his mother Sophia in the realm above him. It was however, the voice of the Ineffable

One. Then he saw a brilliant light through the veil separating him from the realms above, and in that light he saw a figure of a perfect human being through the veil. This was the Son of Humanity, the Christ, but Yaldabaoth did not know it.

It was then, Yaldabaoth, along with his authorities, chose to create a human being resembling what he saw through the veil, in hopes that this being would be able to give all of them the power of light, since it came from above where his mother and all the Light beings reside. So, "they created a being like the first perfect human and said, 'Let's call it Adam that its name may give us power of light" (Nag Hammadi).

They created a material man, but imperfect and without life. The material body of this man was created by all the authorities of Yaldabaoth, each creating one aspect of the human body in their likenesses. Likeness meaning their passions, virtues or vices. As for the breathing of life into Adam: Sophia prayed to the Ineffable One to take back the Light she mistakenly and sorrowfully surrendered to her creation. Hearing her plea, the All sent five luminaries (angels) down to the realm of Yaldabaoth in order to delude him into giving up his light, stolen from the Mother Sophia. They told Yaldabaoth to breathe some of his spirit into Adam so that his body would rise with animated life.

> He breathed his spirit into Adam. The spirit is the power of his mother, but he did not realize this, because he lives in ignorance. The Mother's power went out of Yaldabaoth and into the physical body that had been made to be like the one who is from the beginning. The body moved and became powerful. And it was enlightened (Nag Hammadi, 125).

We, the human beings of today, are the manifestation of the Ineffable One imbued with the Christ Spirit as soul. When

Yaldabaoth saw how powerful and enlightened Adam was, he and all his minions became envious of their creation's intelligence, light and his lack of darkness. They, after all, were the Creators of Adam so, they took Adam and placed him in the "lowest part of the whole material realm." However, Adam was empowered with "enlightened insight," a gift and helper from the Mother-Father to protect Adam. She instilled within the knowledge of his existence and filled him with light making him whole. Still, humanity would suffer because the Archons deliberately placed a "fetter of forgetfulness . . ." over him and he "became a mortal person." Adam would be the first material human as well as the first being to become alienated from the Ineffable and the immortal realms.

The Bible discloses placing Adam in a paradise, a garden where everything is good and flourishes. Eve, however, was not created through Adam's physical rib. According to the Nag Hammadi Scripture in the Secret Book of John, Yaldabaoth removed part of Adam's power (his rib) and because he knew how to create a human form he created another form in the likeness of a female thinking this female would be the darkness such as they were. This figure was bestowed with the power taken from Adam and, in fact, also became Enlightened Insight or Eve, the power given to Adam to protect him. We shall speak more of Eve's origin below.

We know that in the garden were placed two trees: the Tree of Life and the Tree of Knowledge. The first human male and female beings were given rule over everything, but were instructed by god (Yaldabaoth), not to eat of the Tree of Knowledge ". . . thou shalt surely die."

Now, Yaldabaoth placed two trees in the garden. He told Adam to eat freely of the tree of their Life, placed in the middle of Paradise. Yaldabaoth hoped to snare Adam and have him become one of darkness; for this tree was the tree of Life in chaos, of which Yaldabaoth is the ruler. "The dwelling place of those who taste of it is the underworld, and darkness is their resting place" (Nag Hammadi).

The Archons blocked the Tree of Knowledge from Adam's view. This tree is really Enlightened Insight. It was the Christ who came to Adam so that he may be full with the knowledge of the Upper realms.

> "I [John] said to the Savior, 'Lord, was it not the serpent that instructed Adam to eat?'" "The Savior...said, 'The serpent instructed them to eat of the wickedness of sexual desire and destruction so that Adam might be of use to the serpent....For me, I appeared in the form of an eagle upon the tree of knowledge which is the Insight of pure enlightened Forethought, that I might teach the human beings and awaken them from the depth of their sleep... Insight appeared to them as light and awakened their minds." (Nag Hammadi. 126, 127).

It was the authorities who created the beasts of the earth. They created reptiles, birds and all sorts of animals in their likenesses. Because the seven Archons are of matter, they created humans of matter like themselves, but with the form of the human being that appeared to them through the veil of the aeon above, the Christ. In some doctrines the Christ is also known as the "Adam of Light" (Nag Hammadi). Adam was or is the prototype for all humans, both man and woman. However, many likenesses of the First Human were created on the earth yet molded by the Archons. (Inner Christianity). This too may account for the science of humans throughout our evolution beginning as primitive cave dwellers: the Denisovans and Neanderthals, and then Homo sapiens.

Eve, however, was the creation of the Mother of All called "Eve of Life," the "female instructor of Life" (Nag Hammadi). The tree of Life, according to the Orthodox bible, was readily available to Adam and Eve and they were told to eat freely thereof. However, the Tree of Knowledge was forbidden, lest they both die. (Genesis).

> And out of the ground made the Lord God to grow every tree that is pleasant to the sight, and good for food; the tree of life also in the midst of the garden and the tree of knowledge of good and evil (King James Bible, Genesis. 2:9).

It was the serpent, a messenger of the true God, the Ineffable, who came to them exclaiming that they should eat of the tree of knowledge so their eyes would be opened, and yes, they did eat (Richard Smoley, Genesis). The serpent or "beast" according to Gnostic scripture is the "Instructor," Eve of Life (Nag Hammadi). "If all symbols are really functions and signs of things imbued with energy, then the serpent or snake is, by analogy, symbolic of energy itself—of [creative] force pure and simple…" (A Dictionary of Symbols. J. E. Cirlot. 285). As well, if you know anything about the Chakras, you will find that the root chakra houses the Kundalini, symbolized by the snake rising through the spine up into the crown of the head. The snake is simply symbolic of energy flowing.

According to Richard Smoley in Inner Christianity, it is the biblical God, Yaldabaoth, who has lied to Adam and Eve. Their eyes were indeed opened, however, they were opened to gnosis.

The Nag Hammadi Scriptures: *On the Origin of the World*, proclaims the tree of Knowledge causes the soul to awaken from its trance inflicted by the Archons in order that they might eat of it and obtain eternal Life. This tree, as opposed to being placed in the midst of the garden was placed in the "north of Paradise." North may be taken as above Paradise, another realm or dimension. Another benefit in eating of this tree's fruits is that they would condemn the Archons and all their minions. In Nag Hammadi, *Three Forms of First Thought*, of humans who eat of the tree of eternal life, The Ineffable Mother, Protennoia says,

> . . . I explained to those who are mine, who are the children of light, so that they might nullify them all, be liberated from all bonds, and return to the place where they were in the beginning. . . the spirit in the soul, which came from the water of life (727).

The children of humankind, the human beings on earth, the descendants of Seth or the Adam of Light (the Christ) are all endowed with the Light of the Ineffable Mother, Ineffable Father and Ineffable Son. It is this Light that allows us to ascend to the higher aeons once we are endowed with Gnosis. It is our mission on earth to obtain Gnosis/Divine Knowledge and become that which we once were. Each of us has the spark of knowing. It is up to us whether we turn on the light or stay in the dark.

*"Truth be told, Truth be heard, Truth be thrown away.
It's easier to believe the Dogma of the churches and temples
than to believe your own Soul."*
Dr. Sandy Range

CHAPTER SIX

The Christ Being

Now, concerning the history of the Christ on earth. For now we shall begin with the current or more popular literature of the Bible regarding Jesus, whom this writing will henceforth refer to his Hebrew name as Yeshua the Christ. We know that Yeshua was a child prodigy regarding matters of Spirit. At the age of twelve He taught in the temples preaching a more profound truth to the Rabbis, elders and learned teachers of Jerusalem. "And all that heard Him were astonished . . ." (King James Bible, Luke 2:47). It was the Magi who innocently informed Herod about Yeshua during their search for the whereabouts of the birth of this king. We know that Herod would not want any competition to his authority as king over Jerusalem.

In a dream, Joseph, the Child's father, understood that Yeshua was in danger. He took Mary, the birth mother, and the Child into Egypt in order to flee Herod who sought to remove and destroy the would-be "...King of the Jews."(KJB. Matthew 2:2). "Arise and take the young child and his mother, and flee into Egypt (2:13)...When he arose, he took the young child and his mother by night and departed to Egypt."(2:14)

Biblical scripture doesn't tell us what happened to Yeshua during the termed lost years from twelve years of age until His return to Galilee at the age of thirty (there or about). We only know that once

Yeshua returned from Egypt and came into Nazareth, John the Baptist is suddenly on the scene and Yeshua presents himself, as an adult, to be baptized by him.

However, according to Yogi Ramacharaka in *Mystic Christianity*, Yeshua spent time, as a child, studying with various Masters of the Essene Brotherhood: the Magi, while traveling through India, Persia and Egypt. It was the same Magi that greeted Yeshua at his birth with gifts that assisted in arousing the curiosity of the "mystical brotherhoods in the East. They recognized Yeshua's spiritual intellect, maturity and knowledge and pleaded with his parents to allow them to teach the young boy.

During those missing years Yeshua spent a year or two with each of the various Brotherhoods. They taught him and eventually initiated him into their Brotherhoods. It is said that Yeshua, between twentyone and twentyeight or twentynine years old traveled "among the Brahmans, Buddhists and Zoroastrians," along with lengthy routes through India, Persia and Egypt ministering and teaching truths that caused opposition among the priesthoods. He preached namely against "priestcraft . . . formalism . . .cast . . .distinctions and restrictions . . . seeking to lead the people away from ceremonies and back to Spirit" (Mystic Christianity).

Among the caste classifiers of India Yeshua was branded a troublemaker. Being true to the Spirit within Him Yeshua lived among the lower castes and He was looked upon as a Master by the lower castes and revered for His enlightened teachings (Mystic Christianity).

Now, Annie Besant, in her book *Esoteric Christianity* tells us more about Yeshua's preparation for His adult works. She states that at the age of nineteen years Yeshua received Occult training from an "Essene Monastery near Mount Serbal" where many learned travelers passing from the East would visit. Many of the occult lessons in supernatural, mystical and magical beliefs, practices, and phenomena He received were of Indian and Himalayan origin.

After one year of training with the Essenes Yeshua was promoted from initiate to disciple while in Egypt. Yeshua, still a human, was born with the Ineffable Light already within Him, but now we are able to understand the advanced occult knowledge and wisdom of Yeshua during His childhood, young adulthood and teaching tenure throughout His short adult life.

John the Baptist had prophesied the coming of the Christ (King James Bible), although he did not know who that would be. He was told by his own teachers in the Essenic Brotherhood that "a great Master from foreign parts would join him later on and he, John, should prepare the people for His coming." (Mystic Christianity). After returning to His own country Yeshua was informed of the works of John the Baptist and then decided that John's work was also the work He, Himself would seek to engage in.

Most people today will shun the idea of a Yeshua who was not born of a physiological Virgin Mary (Mystic Christianity) and who was not, from His birth, a God or the God He was to become. In "Esoteric Christianity," we learned from the teachings of the ancient Essene Brotherhoods how Yeshua was already a special child, endowed with advanced knowledge of spiritual matters, however, it wasn't until he was baptized, another Essenic custom, that Yeshua came into His Divine Power as a manifest emanation of the original Creator force. "It is taught that He was taken into India and Egypt and Persia, and other far regions, living for several years at each important center, and being initiated into the various brotherhoods, orders, and bodies having their headquarters there" (Mystic Christianity). Here again, we may understand where Yeshua was during the lost years.

Taken, with consent of his parents after they had been made to understand the significance of their child's advanced knowledge and understanding of Spiritual matters, a group of traveling Magi returned to their own lands with Yeshua where "He might receive instructions for which His soul craved, and for which His mind was fitted" (Mystic Christianity). During His adolescence Yeshua traveled through Egypt, India and Persia (now Iran) where He studied with the great Masters of occultism and esotericism. It was this teaching apprenticeship and finally His discipleship that made Yeshua a Mystic, a Magi and a teacher extraordinaire.

Upon Yeshua's return with His family to Galilee they made their home in Nazareth (Matthew 2:23). Biblical scripture does not provide details of Yeshua's actions immediately after the time of his settlement in Nazareth, but we know He sought out John the Baptist, his own cousin, to baptize him in the Jordan River. "And immediately, on coming up from the water he saw the heavens open and the Spirit, as a dove, descending and remaining upon Him" (Mark 1:9).

Upon His baptism by John the Baptist, Yeshua was anointed with the Holy Fire of the original Spirit, that of the Absolute, the Eternal flame of the Ineffable All that Is. The Origin Spirit or light energy descending within the physical, human, mortal Yeshua, allowed Him to come into His true Self as Master and Teacher of Spiritual Truths. Actually we might understand that the Christ Being possessed Yeshua's human, mortal form and had then become the begotten Son or emanation of the Ineffable. It allowed Yeshua to perform His miracles of feeding masses, healing the sick, waking the dead, walking on water and so much more. "To that manifested Presence the name of 'the Christ' may rightly be given, and it was He who lived and moved in the form of the man Yeshua…" (Mystic Christianity). However, even in this day and time period there are many Christians that do not understand how or even believe that Yeshua could perform such miracles.

So, what makes sense, that Yeshua was born of an unmarried virgin woman and birthed into physical form as a God? "She was found with child of the Holy Ghost…" (Mathew 1:18). Or that through the baptism He was born of the virgin, pure, untouched Spirit of the Absolute, Ineffable God? For when He was needed to receive the Holy Christ Spirit through Baptism He became the Ineffable begotten Son manifest in the physical form of Yeshua. "The man Yeshua yielded himself a willing sacrifice, 'offered himself without spot' to the Lord of Love, who took unto Himself that pure form as tabernacle and dwelt for three years of mortal life." (Esoteric Christianity, 69).

During Yeshua's baptism we may surmise that this "dove" descending upon Him was not really a flesh and blood bird as depicted in so many biblical works of art, but a powerful form of divine energy as light, and manifesting as substance that could be seen and witnessed. "The spirit of God descending like a dove, and lighting upon him" (Matthew 3:16). This descent of the Holy presence of the Ineffable Son, the Adam of Light or the Christ was born in physical, human form within the body of Yeshua. Divine Christhood became manifest. He came into His Being, the manifest emanation of the Absolute, able to perform miraculous works and teach the true wisdom and Gnosis of the soul and spirit to humanity on earth.

In order to better understand what is meant by 'emanation of the Absolute,' let us first describe what an emanation is. Emanation is "of something abstract, but perceptible to originate from a source (Oxford Dictionary online)." The Absolute is one name for God as defined by humankind's limited understanding of God. "In religious philosophy, the Absolute is the concept of a form of Being which transcends limited, conditional, everyday existence (Wikipedia)."

Yeshua's teachings to his disciples and to the masses (Teachings on the Mount) were parables or stories of right living and right life. He gave us, according to the Bible, the Way to salvation through faith, living a just and rightly life, and through unwavering faith in the eternal God. The Bible gives us prayers and songs of repentance and mercy. It tells us how to ask for forgiveness. It gives us the stories of the few who travelled with Yeshua that reveal the hardships they endured that we are to learn from.

What the Bible does not give us is the esoteric meanings of the stories. In Mark 4:11 Christ discloses to His disciples, ". . . Unto you it is given to know the mystery of the kingdom of God; but unto them that are without all these *things* are done in parables." Here, we have those who are within. These are the inner circle, the disciples of the Christ who receive the esoteric or inner teachings that are not given to the masses. The exoteric or outer circle of people were taught through stories because most were not ready to receive those inner teachings. Even of the apostles there were a few who were not able to understand yet they were provided a glimpse of the inner workings of the aeons and how we might ascend to the realms from which we originated.

In the Nag Hammadi Scriptures, The Secret Book of James tell us that the Christ returned "Five hundred fifty days, after he rose from the dead" and stayed among them for eleven years (Pistis Sophia). During these eleven years Christ taught the disciples of the Mysteries of His realm and of those of the invisible regions. The disciples he spoke to were more than the twelve and included women, a few being Mary Magdalene, Mary, Yeshua's birth mother and Martha among others.

The Truth about Mary Magdalene.

The bible also tells part of the story, although skewed in its accuracy, that of Mary Magdalene or Miriam of Magdala. This Mary was one of Christ's most astonishing disciples. Because the times of her day diminished women, she stood out even among her peers, the 12 men disciples, as the most learned of Christ's teachings.

When the Christ had departed from his disciples for the last time they were all in fear that they too would be crucified, tortured and put to death while preaching and teaching the Christ's Word. It was Mary Magdalene who came forward and comforted them: "Do not weep and be distressed nor let your hearts be irresolute. For his grace will be with you all and will shelter you" (Nag Hammadi).

How is it, this mere woman follower of Christ is exemplified above all her brethren? When the Christ was speaking to the disciples of great mysteries not disclosed before, Mary would ask many explicit questions of the Master in order that she and her brethren understood fully and completely the deeply complex mysteries revealed by the Christ. He obliged her each and every time. Mary said to Christ after hearing him speak, "My Lord, my indweller of light hath ears and I comprehend every word which thou sayest" (Pisits Sophia). She goes on to explain her understanding to the Christ who ". . .was greatly astonished at the definitions of the words which she spake, for she had become pure spirit utterly . . .(114).

It may seem as if the Christ favored Mary above the other disciples in his commentary to her stating he will bless and perfect her even more than the other disciples (Pistis Sophia). However the relationship between Mary and the Christ may appear, Mary was the most learned disciple of Christ and understood the esoteric meaning of all His teachings of the mysteries in a greater capacity than her brethren disciples. Is it no wonder that Peter was jealous and had disdain for Miriam of Magdala.

In the same period of conversation where Mary asked the Christ many questions, Peter interrupts and complains to the Christ that Mary has taken up too much of their (disciples) time and he refuses to allow her to keep speaking. Christ responds with "Let him in whom the power of his spirit shall seethe, so that he understandeth what I say, come forward and speak" (Pistis Sophia).

After a time Christ again, clothed in His vestures of the Light of the Ineffable, ascended back to his realm, but not before revealing the way home for all humankind on this earth (Pistis Sophia, in entirety).

In reviewing the above, we might surmise that the Nag Hammadi scriptures are full with writings of a people who were opposed to the orthodox Christian leaders of their time. Yet, how do we know these writers weren't really on to something? Both the Bible and the Nag Hammadi Scriptures have many similarities and even some of the same writers: Paul, James, Peter and John. The Nag Hammadi has even more books from familiar biblical characters such as Phillip, Thomas and Mary Magdalene among other known and lesser acknowledged personalities. We also know that Mary Magdalene wrote her own book that was never included in the Orthodox Christian Bible.

The Gnostic Christian reality of the Ineffable God and the creation of the heavens, earth and humankind may appear to be imaginary. However, the bible's version of the creation story may also appear to be imaginary. The bible does not tell us of the creation of the heavens and the abodes of both the upper immortal aeons of light and the lower heavens that include the abyss or hell. However, what may appear more feasible is the Gnostic explanation of the one true Ineffable God, and how He came to look upon His own reflection to create an emanation of Himself as both the Eternal Mother, the feminine aspect of Himself, and the Begotten Son, God Himself as substance. This appears a feasible story of the initial or first creations from which all other creations came into being.

What we know from the Gnostic scriptures is that the Ineffable God is not the Creator god, Yaldabaoth. The Gnostic Christians considered Yaldabaoth the god of Moses who was jealous and vengeful. Would the one true Ineffable God be so jealous and vengeful? Would that God require human and animal sacrifices, human suffering, slavery, torture and imprisonment in his name? The Ineffable God, in this writer's opinion, is a loving God seeking to teach humans the way back home, the way back to Him. Of course, He also gave us free will and choice, but He sent His emissary to guide us back home and it is up to us to follow that path.

Richard Smoley reports that the fall of humanity is the result of Adam and Eve being given what they desired, first-hand knowledge (gnosis), of both good and evil, by way of direct experience. Therefore they were removed from Paradise, an other-dimensional reality, and sent into material reality, the earth. Smoley continues to assess how the Gnostics designed a spiritual belief comprised of two gods: One inferior: Yaldabaoth and one Omnipotent: The Ineffable God.

Who were the Gnostics? Elaine Pagels writes in an article for PBS, "The term nosticism. . .an umbrella term to cover people that the leaders of the church don't like." She goes on to say that the rise of priests, bishops and deacons nearing the end of the second century, professed to speak for all Christians and any viewpoints to the contrary of the bishops' rule was labeled precariously heretical. In fact, if you were a Christian Gnostic you "belonged to an illegal movement" and were sought out, rounded up, tried for heresy, persecuted and murdered publicly (Pagels).

Pagels reports that Christians who did not conform to the new laws imposed by the church leaders, laws that the Christ Himself told His disciples not to create or impose, were severely punished by imprisonment, torture and even death. She goes on to explain that in their time, the early Christians, Gnostic and otherwise, were exceptionally divided in their beliefs and religious customs. The Church, however, attempts to establish structure and bring the followers of Christ under one roof.

A new, young Bishop, Irenaeus, who was between 18 and 20 years old, along with his priests decided which books, writings, rituals and teachings should be customary and appropriate for the new Christian Church. (Pagels). Today we have too many Christian denominations with a wide assortment of rituals, customs and interpretations of Christ's teachings. It appears modern Christianity has lost the meaning of Christ and more so, has lost His Spirit.

Were the Gnostics wrong to believe what they did? Even today, in this enlightened time and space of intellectualism, there are mainstream Christian religious communities that still persist with the notions that the Gnostics are heretics and devil worshipers that should be burned at the stake. Just as there are many different denominations, beliefs and rituals among today's Christians, so too were the Gnostics in their beliefs and rituals. What we, today, do not realize is that the Gnostics are very much like mainstream Christianity. The difference is in the content of the books and scriptures written by the Gnostics.

We might also find argument against the authenticity of the Nag Hammadi texts from Douglas Groothuis in "The Gnostic Gospels: Are They Authentic:" Groothuis relies upon one of the contributors to the Nag Hammadi Scriptures, James Robinson, to make his point:

> "...the texts were translated one by one from Greek to Coptic, and not always by translators capable of grasping the profundity or sublimity of what they sought to translate..." most of the texts are adequately translated, and that when there is more than one version of a particular text, the better translation is clearly discernable. Nevertheless, he is "led to wonder about the bulk of the texts that exist only in single version," because these texts cannot be compared with other translations for accuracy.

Duly noted. However, we will find that Robinson simply wrote the Preface to the Nag Hammadi Scriptures and had no part in its translations or editing. As well, Groothuis neglects, in the above comments, to note the massive book burnings of the original writers' texts by the early church, Irenaeus in particular. And, Mystical literature such as the Nag Hammadi and Dead Sea Scrolls that were found buried in caves or in the ground over hundreds of years, have been eroded away, lost or burned as kindling for cooking fires before they were turned over to scholars and museums. Imagine what will be found in the future to enlighten us on our path to ascension.

If Irenaeus became bishop at about 177 AD (Early Church. Web), and he adamantly set upon a mission to destroy all Gnostic books and believers in his time, would it not be suffice to say that the Gnostics had the same, although different, separate and maybe superior knowledge of Yeshua as did the orthodox Christians?

One might make an argument that the original and early writings of the Christian Gnostics, that included the apostles of Christ, were destroyed as heresy because Irenaeus, himself, found the secret teachings of Christ to His disciples hard to believe or he refused to give credit to those writers because they opposed him. Was there jealousy and piousness involved? Even Peter, Christ's disciple upon who the Christian church was supposedly founded, was jealous of the knowledge and love bestowed upon others of Christ's disciples, especially that of Mary Magdalene.

We should remember there were many denominations of Gnostics and Christians during that era, and all were vehemently sought out and threatened with imprisonment, torture and/or death if they did not submit to the church fathers' proposals of doctrine and ritual.

It was the sacred and unbound teachings of the Gnostics that Irenaeus and his brotherhood of priests and bishops feared. Unfortunately, for the Gnostic Christians, Irenaeus won the fight for the books to be included in the bible. We should also remember that this early church was the founding of the Roman Catholic church of which has an appalling history of torture, murder and imprisonment in the name of Christ, of those who did not believe as they did. "Irenaeus is the leading representative of Catholic Christianity in the last quarter of the second century, the champion of orthodoxy against Gnostic heresy. . . ." (Early Church. Web).

We should also remember that, even today, the Vatican has a vast library of ancient texts and they deny access to the general public and even researchers for scholastic endeavors. How do we know that many of the early Gnostic texts are not behind these secured walls forever hidden from all of us?

Scott Bidstrup, *The Case Against the Case for Christ*, interviews with various "Christian Apologists," relating inconsistencies with the Canonical Gospels of the Bible. In an interview with Craig Bloomberg, Ph.D., senior researcher and currently at Denver Seminary, Bidstrup reports questions on the authorship of the gospels.

> Bloomberg claims that Matthew, Mark and Luke, all apostles of Jesus, were the authors of the gospels attributed to them is entirely unsupported...His assertion is contraindicated by many other scholars, both apologetic and secular. The claims that "Papias, writing in 125 AD" verifies the authorship of Mark, and that Mark recorded events accurately, is fundamentally without merit. It's as meaningful and as useful as my personally telling you, more than a century after the time of Joseph Smith [Latter Day Saints], that "yeah, the guy really did dig up some more golden plates, and yeah, the Book of Mormon is an accurate translation of them." Papias is as distant from the events he's verifying as I am from the events of Joseph Smith's time. So why should we believe him?

Bidstrup makes an excellent point in his interview with Bloomberg.

Purportedly, the Christian canonical gospels are stated as fact, truth, to be read and believed literally without question. With an eye for discernment and a little comparison we can see that even the books of the bible are not entirely accurate. We should also understand that there were many translators and editors within the early Orthodox Church and the English King James version of the Bible, completed in 1611, was not the first translation.

According to Margaret Mowczko in *7 Things You May Not Know about the King James Bible* (web), she tells us not only did this first English translation contain the unpopular Apocryphal texts among the Protestant majority of the time. These texts were removed in the 1666 edition. King James charged his translators to throw out the Puritan's popular Geneva Bible due to its commentaries in the margins. It "did not show respect for kings." As well, King James ordered the new translation to "keep words that supported a bishop led hierarchy." His last order was that only his version of the bible would be read in England's churches. (Mowczko).

From the *Boston College School of Theology, Profile: The Gospel of Matthew*, we find that Matthew, sometime around the year 70 AD, competes with Jewish scholars of the Torah for influence. Thought mostly containing Jewish members, the Gentile members of his congregation are "expected to obey Torah norms. . . including circumcision." This report further states that Matthew's Gospel is organized for instructional purposes. It contains five sermons of Jesus . . .that recall the five books of the Torah." From the gospel of Luke, the church is failing among the Jewish community. However, it is growing steadfastly among the gentiles. Many questions arose among the Jews regarding God's promise to them. "If blessing through Christ was now shifting onto Gentiles, what did that say about divine promises to Jews? Or was the church a heretical deviation from Judaism as some were charging." (Boston College School of Theology. Web.)

The Boston College research reports on many discrepancies in the so-called factual reports of the gospels. Here we have two different accounts of Yeshua's parents and birth. "Luke reports that Joseph and Mary, the parents of Yeshua, were both from Galilee who fled because of the census into Bethlehem. Matthew's report, however, is that the family is originally from Bethlehem and upon their return from Egypt, to where they fled because of Herod, settled in Galilee. (Boston College).

So, we can see many discrepancies in the books of the bible just as we see them in the Nag Hammadi scriptures. However, since many of the books written both from Gnosticism and Christianity had been destroyed it will be difficult to know the whole truth.

This chapter's intent was to give the reader a different perspective on the Christian story of our creation and the creation of the universe. The Gnostic and Orthodox Christian stories basically tell the same story, but from different points of view and experience. The Gnostic view, in this writer's opinion, provides an expanded view, fills in many gaps and tells us what we may never know about the Universe and its many realms of Being and existence if we are glued to the King James Bible.

In this day and age, here in the 21st Century, there are many who are discovering or channeling information from Divine Masters, Angels, and other Light Beings that tell us of our own divinity. We are receiving messages that inform us how to transform from within, release past karma and evolve spiritually. The Nag Hammadi Scriptures show us the universe before conception into physical reality. It tells us with vivid detail how the Ineffable God manifested Himself as Divine mind (creative thought), as Divine Feminine or Mother and the Son, Christ. It further explains how each Being of Light manifested in its realm from the Divine Feminine as Barbelo in the Ineffable realm. And what we can also discern and acknowledge is the masculine (Ineffable God/Father) and feminine (Ineffable God/Mother) energies. Father Mother God are one in the same.

The power of creation was given to the Beings in the Treasury of Light, in pairs, to further manifest other Beings of Light. What we might discover from this is a hierarchy of Beings and realms. We came forth from these realms of Light.

The further away these realms were created from the Source, the less Light was available to them. This made these beings among the far lower realms fallible. They made mistakes and possessed virtues that were less than desirable in the eyes of the Ineffable and the Treasury of Light. Yet, the Ineffable had a plan to include and utilize all these creations good, bad and indifferent.

We also learned that Yaldabaoth, because of his inadequacies and ignorance created humans without life. It was through Sophia and the Christ Being that life was breathed into human beings and gave us a soul, making us perfect. Yet, Yaldabaoth, in his jealousy, created a veil of forgetfulness over us so that *we could not remember from where we originated*. It is our purpose to remember from whence we came and to turn within, live accordingly in our Divinity so we may return home.

We know that Yeshua was born a man, although predestined to become the Christ or the Ineffable God manifest in physical form. Upon his baptism the Christ spirit filled Yeshua and He became the anointed one, the God-Self manifest. What he taught humanity in His day has been distorted and undermined by many of the Christian churches of His day and ours.

What the Christ came to teach us is, indeed, in the King James Bible and the Nag Hammadi Scriptures. We have to learn to read these scriptures with a discerning eye. We need to know and understand the esoteric or inner meaning of the lessons the Christ taught us. He came to teach us that we, every one of us, has the same innate power and knowledge to do the same works as He. He taught us that we are cosmic beings, descendants of the Treasury of Light, the First Aeon. If we can turn within and dedicate our minds to Spirit we can overcome the veil of forgetfulness and remember our Divinity in its true form.

What the Nag Hammadi Scriptures reveal is a treasury of esoteric knowledge. The talks given by the Christ to His disciples, that included five women, reveal teachings not written about in the

Orthodox Christian Bible. We also find that the Christ returned to our earth after His resurrection and remained for eleven years with His disciples. He taught them the mysteries of the afterlife and the heavenly realms. He revealed the knowledge of the powers to heal, to manifest what we need and desire in life: to become as He was, a living, breathing Christ on earth.

He also taught that the true God-Self within each of us can be accessed with the practice of right living and devotion to Spirit. However, that devotion must be sincere and practiced in our lives each and every day, at all times awake and asleep in our dreams. It means putting away all prejudice. It means total acceptance of all others and circumstances. It means constant prayer and meditation in order to raise our consciousness and live our divinity in a manner directed by the Holy Spirit on auto-pilot. It is these lessons that the Christ as Yeshua came to teach us. It is within the Christ spirit that we are to learn how to get back home. We are here to experience life as emissaries of the Ineffable. To ensure that we learn, grow and evolve to become that which we once were.

You, the reader should do your own investigation into the Nag Hammadi Scriptures, the Pistis Sophia and other Gnostic works. Take what resonates into your heart and discard the rest or let it seed for a later time when you are ready to nurture it.

So, is your head spinning? When I first began studying these ancient scriptures it made my head spin too! No worries. What we all want is to become that Christ spirit within again so we can make our ascension. Being a Christ Spirit has nothing to do with race, religion or any other belief system. It has to do with Getting Your Soul Right! I actually had this tattooed as *Get Your Soul Right*.

I once heard someone say, 'Eternity is confined whereas Infinity is both before and after time. This is so true. If we can think of ourselves as being Infinite, we are acknowledging our Divinity and Oneness with the Ineffable One. After all, is not the one true immeasurable God Infinite, both before and after time? So are we.

I understand the previous two chapters may have been a little difficult to read, especially for devout Christians, however, they play an important part in your understanding of who we are as human and divine beings.

Wow! So did you learn anything? Are you totally confused? Are you P.O.'d? Your honest answers to these questions will tell what frequency you are vibrating at. Only you can know this. No judgements if you're not yet ready. It happens. Just keep moving forward. All of you!

> "Connect with the core of your being.
> That eternal flame of life that burns within.
> Ignite the fire. Fan the flames."
> Dr. Sandy Range

CHAPTER SEVEN

The Road to Transformation

The "Light" in Enlightenment

I was speaking with some colleagues a few days ago and the subject of becoming enlightened came up. What I discovered is that there are many interpretations of enlightenment. Some see it as advanced knowledge or gnosis. Some see it as grace or being filled with the Holy Spirit. Some see it as reaching Nirvana or the release and freedom of all things worldly. Some even see it as an awakening and merging with the Divine.

All of the above definitions of Enlightenment are true and, I am sure, there are many more. However, we might look at Enlightenment in the sense of being awake or super-consciously aware. If the human mind is limitless, then we might say everyone is enlightened, but to the degree that one is aware of one's conscious and super-conscious potential and uses it. Again, gnosis!

In my humble opinion, my studies and practices have led me to prefer to think of Enlightenment as something spiritual, divine, filled with the Light of the All, the Ineffable One. The Light itself is beyond the comprehension of the human mind. In fact the word itself "Light" in human terms is simply deficient of its true meaning. The Light in Enlightenment may signify the becoming of something more than mere human. Becoming something divine, holy, spiritual, and pure. This Light of the All is a Light that blinds or awakens, cripples or heals, defeats or empowers and so much more according to one's will or lack thereof.

How do we find enlightenment? By turning inward. When we use our inner eyes to see the truth about ourselves and be honest about our transgressions, mistakes, willful harm, hurtful thoughts about others, bad deeds, etc. throughout our lifetime, we become humbled or become more angry (ego). In becoming humbled, we shouldn't beat ourselves up, but ask for forgiveness from our maker, from ourselves, and those who may have suffered because of us even if we were not aware of it.

For some this is an extremely difficult task to complete, and even more difficult to be honest with one's self in recognizing and acknowledging our faults and faulty actions (ego). If, however, one is able to accomplish this purging with true sincerity, and one truly forgives one's self, know that true forgiveness has been granted. Simply accept it. Don't dwell on it!

When a deep, heart-felt forgiveness is realized, and it must be realized, a great burden is lifted from us. We experience true freedom. What happens next? The Light is already within us. It is in our consciousness, our minds and our hearts. Once the burden of our transgressions is lifted and released, and as long as we choose life and light for our lives, looking upward (from within) we engage the Light of Enlightenment. It is up to each of us to embrace that Light, to cause that Light to grow and dwell within us. When we become free, when we become knowledgeable about the Light and its Source, when we are able to live in a manner that is of pureness in thought, deed and practice then Enlightenment is achievable.

But what about love?

Well, love is the quintessential necessity of life. Without love, there is no human condition that can be healed, held together, made whole or completed. Love is what we, as human beings are.

No matter how sad, glum, desperate, angry or hurt we may feel, deep down there is a little pocket of Light that is filled with the Love of the Ineffable All that Is. That love is immeasurable. It is the Light that keeps us afloat and moving forward. It keeps us alive!

Tapping into that Light and Love, acknowledging its presence within us brings us to a place of peace. When we can affectively relate to accepting peace, we can inevitably accept love. After acceptance of love comes faith and after faith comes knowing or gnosis!

Knowing who we are deep within and all throughout is being the Love and Light of the Ineffable All that Is manifest in physical form. We become the Light to which everything is made of, and understand our connection to all things animate and inanimate. We become a magnet for good and others are able see and feel that Light. They too want to know what that is and we, emanating our Love and Light, can show them.

This is how we heal ourselves, our families, our communities and our world. Tap into that little pocket of Light within. Allow it to take you over. Allow it to grow and evolve into something magnificent. You know it's there. You feel it even though you may be feeling the shadows of dark emotions. The dark emotions are simply the ego's temper tantrum. Not getting its way, placing conditions on everyone and everything and seeking immediate gratification is the ego's attempt to control everything and when it does not get its way it has a temper tantrum! Who suffers? We do! Each of us individually and those around us.

Tune into the Light and Love of the Ineffable within you. It brings true joy to the heart and mind. It allows us to shine from within and provides nourishment for the soul to accomplish anything we desire. What's Love got to do with it? Everything! It is who we are.

Knowing who we are, knowing that we are the children of the Universe, even tapping into the Light of the Source is only a start. Here's the deal! If we are not consistently in a state of love for everything and everyone, yes, even the creepy crawlers and the creepy people, then we have not met the mark. Constant love is having the ability and the will to love everything and everyone unconditionally. We must morph into a state of perpetual love for all things. Love is the source of our being. It is who and what we really are. We need, more than anything else, including food and water, to be the love of the world. Then, everything else will come to us.

Walking the Red Road.

In Indigenous North America, we do what is called "Walking the Red Road." In Native America the Red Road is the path we walk in this lifetime. It is a way of being and living in the world where we are connected to all things in Creation. In this way we live with integrity, honor, confidence, compassion and respect. The Red Road is spiritual, emotional, mental and physical. It is a life long journey, ever learning, ever growing, ever evolving to live in total balance and harmony with all that is. It is a gift to us from our ancestors and our dutiful gift to the next seven generations.

Because we are each connected we must learn to walk strongly, yet with tender foot. We must live with honor and integrity and be fully aware of the footprint we are leaving along the path. It is to look for beauty in all things. In this way we walk in balance with the earth, the sky and all things within the Circle of Life. The Red Road path is a sacred, healing path for the mind, spirit, body and emotions. Walking the **Red Road** is a life long journey…ever learning…ever growing…

ever evolving. The **Red Road** Pathway is a method for living in the world where healing takes place and all things are possible.

==Everything in Creation is Sacred. We recognize and acknowledge that everything on this earth, above it, below it, within it and surrounding it is a gift of the Great Spirit: The two-leggeds, the four-leggeds, the swimming ones, the flying ones, the creeping and crawling ones are all Sacred. The plant people, the tree people, the stone people are sacred. The elementals and spirits of fire, air, earth and water are all sacred. …and…ALL… are our relatives… All are our family… We are all connected one to the other.==

Have you ever thought about the impact you will leave for your own children seven generations from now? Profound isn't it? Will they have a healthy world to live in? Maybe and maybe not. If we, the human species, the species with the (allegedly) highest intelligence, do not make changes now, we may not have anything to leave our descendants. Not only that, but it is up to every single one of us to make that change. The change is made within the Self!

In every culture there are ancient traditions that honor and respect the cosmos, the Universe and the powers that created it. Each of us, no matter where we came from originally have a rich cultural history running through our DNA. It's not only in our physical DNA either. It runs through our Soul DNA, the substance of what we are made of in spirit. Tune in to your Soul knowing and you *will* feel it. You will know it.

==If you tune in to your Soul knowing you will feel, you will know, you will recognize the Light in your Enlightenment.== The rich cultural heritage I spoke of above originates from the place among the stars that we came from. As you become elevated and move into your heart center you also move away from your fear.

Here is a poem I wrote many decades ago. It speaks of the plan the (Ineffable One) Great Spirit or Grandfather has for us, all of us, our human family:

GRANDFATHER'S GIFT

Once long ago in another life we bonded and loved one another
Tender and sweet was that love until we lost our way
The wilderness of the world obstructed our souls' paths
We became lost and hungered, but knew not for what

Then Spirit laid out a new path before us to follow
And the road though long and far was straight and swift
Without hesitation we followed that red road to one another
Heeding the rhythms of our hearts the Spirit drum led us home

Do you feel the knowing, the gnawing in your soul as I do
The voices of our ancestors sing us support and strength
Their power guides us urging us onward ever nearer the truth
Feel the rhythm of their dance in celebration of our becoming

The Spirits manifest miracles within the blessings bestowed
Powerful blood running strong and deep through our veins
Just as our coupling so tied umbilically to Grandmother's womb
Divine is the gift to thee and me to travel Grandfather's path as one

And Grandfather has brought us together in this lifetime once again
We've been given a second chance upon which to build and grow
Let us honor that which has been gifted to us from the Star People
One within the Other, soulful and loved, whole and complete
Trust your heart and I will trust mine for only they speak truth
Let us share of miracles manifest as we walk the red road
Coincidence this is not for this is part of Grandfather's plan
With honor let us not stray, but stay soul mates bonded forever

Tender and sweet is the love we make and share and provide
It strengthens and grows and expands with each encounter
Familiar comfort pervades our senses and our knowing
Familiar... yes familiar are we in becoming once again

Do you know do you sense who we are this time around
Do you feel the tie that binds us heart to heart and soul to soul
Do you remember this feeling this embrace this soulful spirituality
It was not so long ago, but it is here now again for us to complete

And in this sharing and bonding once again we are called
A mission Grandfather has bestowed upon us to complete once more
For there can be no love without love for all Creation
And this is the path the red road we must follow to the end

It is in this that the spirits sing their praises of honor
And in this that they prepare to guide us onward to our end
Whole and complete walking softly with power and might
We are the flame ignited in the hearts of all things

The mission is our purpose for Being in this life
The Peacemaker and the Healer bound as one now fulfilled
Birthed as the children of the star people to make peace
And give hope and to make the world whole again.

This is the truth of who we are, where we must go and how we must behave. We have lost our way, but so many around the world are finding the straight and narrow path to enlightenment. It is only through love that we can raise our frequencies and move into our divinity.

But, I'm afraid!

Remember transformation is change. With change comes fear of the unknown. Start where you are and think of the person you are right now. Connect with and define who you are in this moment. Not who you were in the past. Fear will keep you stuck. All mental disorders and many medical conditions are the results of our long held fears. We can be deeply depressed and feel unfathomable sorrow and pain, but why? Because we are in fear. We fear our family, friends, work, relationships, situations, circumstances, events, animals, trees, you name it, and we will find a way to fear it. When we live in fear for so long we develop new fears. Wake up call, when you know who and what you truly are there is nothing on this earth to fear. We were made to love, not fear!

I get it. I know some of you really do feel hurt and pain and fear. So we might ask: Does Personal Suffering Ever End? It may seem as though once we manage to work through one issue that has caused us to suffer in some way, here comes another. A friend says or does something to us that causes emotional stress and hurt. The boss yells and screams and we feel like we're not worthy or we are a loser. A lover or partner ends the relationship and we feel betrayed and defeated. A family member willfully stones us with his or her words and we experience pain.

All of these scenarios *appear* as though someone else has caused us to feel pain. It *seems* like people are out to get us and we are just sitting ducks for hurtful attacks. How do we respond to these attacks? We usually feel the anger the other person is dishing out and then… we take it all inside of ourselves. We absorb the anger and hurtful words and actions. This causes us to feel varying degrees of pain and anger, hurt and disillusionment. Our minds race with thoughts of the actual incident. We imagine what we could have said or done and this causes us more anguish because we didn't do what we could have done at the time.

Stop! If you've understood what was written above when I wrote: "appear" or "seems," then you know these two verbs denote: "to have the appearance of… "gives the impression of" (Merriam-Webster Dictionary). What this means is we, or rather ego, have the habit of taking on the anger, misery and pain of another person when they say or do something that *appears* to us as threatening or hurtful. The truth is that the other person is in pain, is miserable or angry and they choose to release some of those emotions on whomever is in their path.

It is up to us to recognize that it is the other person's stuff! Allow, permit or give consent to yourself to let that person own their own stuff. It is up to us to recognize that we are not the problem (ego). It is the offending person's problem. The key is to NOT allow ourselves (ego) to absorb their emotions. After all, those emotions belong to the other person and not to us. Don't take ownership! Just be aware, observe, listen, and detach. When we learn to do this we become free.

Awareness Meditation can help you release and detach. It can help you become aware that you are already free and perfect and happy. It is the habits we've accumulated over our many lifetimes that cause our pain. Learning to meditate in Open Awareness can teach us to relieve and transform ourselves to live free and be in total happiness.

What I have learned over my decades on this planet is that humans have a tendency to give in to their fears. *Fear is at the root of all suffering, personal and global.* I'm not one to watch or read the daily news, but one can't help but to be informed by friends, family, colleagues and strangers of the turmoil running amuck in the world. Turmoil, strife, murder, hunger, terrorism, abuse, neglect, attack, assault; you name it, we've got plenty of it. We also have love, compassion, kindness, acceptance, healing, building, helping and more.

Here's the deal. Fear is at the root of all despair and suffering. Fear takes our minds to a place of paranoia and insanity. Fear gives birth to anger, guilt, arrogance, bitterness, envy, obsession, procrastination and countless other negative emotions. When we live in fear, we create, in our minds, the most horrendous outcomes. Our imaginations distort the reality of a situation to become something bigger, badder, and more formidable than it actually is. It creates monsters of things that have already been and those yet to come. Fear is not based in the present moment, where, for the most part, we are in a safe space. It becomes so real in our minds that we *absent-mindlessly* create the circumstances that bring our fears into our reality. What is going on in the world is the result of people's individual fears.

The remedy? Love, kindness and compassion. Both fear and love are choices we make. We can choose to live in fear or we can choose to live with love, kindness and compassion. Make the choice to be free from suffering. Make the choice to live in a manner that promotes kindness and goodwill in self and others. That homeless person you see on the street also wants to be free from suffering. Your obnoxious neighbor wants to be free from suffering. Your colleague or co-worker wants to be free from suffering. Your angry boss wants to be free from suffering…you get the idea. No one wants to suffer and everyone wants to be happy.

When we begin to look at others with better eyes we will see their quest for happiness. They just don't know how to obtain it. We can make a choice to say hello to a stranger, offer a smile, and strike up a conversation. That angry store clerk is suffering. Ask how his or her day is going with a smile. Offer a compliment to your controlling boss. He or she probably never receives compliment. It will make his or her day! Silently bless someone with sincerity and a smile.

There are countless ways we can show love, kindness and compassion to others. The key is to remember that no one wants to suffer and everyone wants to be happy, just like you and me. Use your eyes to see more clearly. Consciously be aware of others' suffering. Look into that antagonist's eyes and see their sorrow. Then take action, in some small or big way, to brighten his or her day! We change the way of the world by starting in our immediate environments. Happiness is contagious!

The happier and freer we become, the more we raise into our higher consciousness and then find enlightenment. Well… we, along with all of the other spiritual super heroes around the world must unite. We must find each other and join forces to bring peace, unity and harmony to the planet!! We are all mirrors for one another. We are all really beginning to connect to each other. Let us reach out with a gentler touch and embrace one another. Welcome home my family!

A Change is Gonna Come

With practice there comes a time on our spiritual paths when we step into another realm of being. The change that takes place feels weird and alien because the spiritual work we do on this plane of existence is felt in many other planes of existence. The Universe takes notice and change happens.

As we learn to release, as we learn to give, as we learn to love openly we are suddenly thrust into a different state of mind and being. At some point we can feel alone, separate and at the same time connected to everything in the universe. Our friends and family don't understand us anymore. Because of this we think that maybe we are going a little crazy and think about returning to our old selves again. Do NOT do it! YOU are not going crazy. You got rid of that egoic behavior remember? You are living as a soul now. That is the purpose! That is your purpose!

This change, this transformation is the next step in our growth and evolution. As we grow spiritually, mindful of every thought and deed, mindful of our speech and our behavior, we become something else. We become something more. Our energy is more vibrant. Our frequencies vibrate higher and faster. We become the Light in the world.

Please do not be frightened of this new way of being or else you will you will lose what you have gained. Instead, turn up the volume of your spirit filled energy and move through the world as spirit would. We all are spirit after all.

Don't worry about family and friends. Sometimes we make the mistake of lowering our vibrations to meet those of the people around us. Instead raise your vibrations and soon those people around you will elevate as well depending on their individual karma.

We are divine beings with a mission on this earth. If you are still struggling with your spirituality seek out an enlightened teacher or holistic therapist to help you. The world itself is changing. You see the upheaval every day. There are powers at work making way for a much bigger change. We are part of that change. YOU are part of that change. It's all about love and evolution!

So now, make it a point to sit in the silence every single day. It's best to sit in the early morning after you rise to set the intention for your day. If you're unable to sit in the morning then you can sit in the silence at night or even during the day if you are at home and the kids are at school or work. So make the time to sit in sanctuary/silence. However you need to get it done is fine as long as you get it done.

"When you shine your own light as the brilliance of the sun, you allow others to shine their light as well. If we all shone our light the whole world could be filled with the brilliance of the human spirit!"
Dr. Sandy Range

CHAPTER EIGHT

Your Intentional Self

Intentionality!!! Being intentional is being deliberate and purposeful. How are you living your life? When we are intentional with our thoughts and words we are better understood. When we are intentional with our actions we accomplish more. When we are intentional with our behaviors we show our true selves. Being intentional in all we do is a way of showing that we are present and aware of ourselves and the world around us.

So let's begin shall we? Let's talk about the many ways we can all be intentional. Some are mentioned above, but we will elaborate on them a little more. Just remember that karma is relative to everything and you will hear me speak about it quite a bit.

Thought Energies

First and foremost being intentional begins in our thoughts. Without thought there is no manifestation of anything. Before anything in the physical world can be created, manufactured, built, etc. it must first be a thought, with an idea of the thing to be created. In the spiritual world thoughts really are things and we need to make sure our thoughts are in alignment with our true nature. Thought is energy just like us! Thoughts are also very powerful tools for either good or bad. We can inflict emotional energetic harm on others through our thoughts or we can surround others with loving, healing, kind thoughts and help them out. Remember, what goes out from you returns to you. That negative harmful thought you just sent your co-worker will come back to you and sooner rather than later! So will the healing loving thought you sent to your neighbor. That is karma. Please make sure your thoughts are in alignment with your true self, your spirit, your soul, your original, higher state of being.

Listening

Listen intentionally all the time. Listening is a skill. We hear people talk to us all the time, but we don't necessarily tune in and really hear them. When we are able to listen effectively and intentionally we are better informed, we better understand, we can repeat back what the person said or at least the key points if a lengthy lecture. Listening honors the person speaking and honors the soul-self by giving your full attention. When we listen intentionally, we are not thinking about our response before the person has finished speaking. It is about effective communication. When you are listening intentionally you are not interrupting the speaker with your own comment or question. You are absorbing the message, the idea, the energy, the purpose of the communication.

Speaking

Speaking is also a skill. It is the cornerstone of our communications with others, with groups, with classes, with whatever. Speaking intentionally involves knowing your own thoughts and carefully communicating what you really want to say. It is knowing and trusting your own mind. If you have to give a speech be mindful of fillers like "um" and "like." This is useful for everyday speech as well. Imagine you were reading this book and in every other sentence you read, "um, pause, okay here's what to do, like ah...." You wouldn't be very happy or want to finish reading this book! Learn to speak intentionally, effectively and clearly. Whomever you are communicating with will be very happy as well and you will be commended for being such an eloquent speaker, not to mention being understood!

Choice & Decision Making

We all know how to make choices and decisions, but many times we are not making intentional choices. We, rather, make choices from the ego's point of view or from a place of desperation. Making intentional choices takes time, awareness and mindfulness. We need to be awake and present in the moment to make an intentional choice. Once we are present we see the conditions we must meet. We see the outcomes clearer. We are informed and knowledgeable about our decisions. Mindless decisions are just that, mind-less, without thought and we reap the results of our faulty and uninformed choices. Now, you can see how ego plays a role in almost every aspect of our lives. The faulty decisions are usually made by ego. Ego is not immune to karma so don't go blaming ego when karma comes around. It was the ego, after all, who listened!

Actions & Behaviors

Your actions speak for you, sometimes above and beyond words. You may have the conscious thought about a situation or know all the right words to say, but if your actions don't show it, it may as well be a lie you just told. We really need to pay close attention to our actions and behaviors and these include facial expressions, eye rolls, looking away when someone is speaking to you. All these behaviors can throw your good intentions right out the window. For every intentional thought, for every intentional decision your behaviors should scream your intentions through the roof. Just be sure they are in alignment with your soul self.

Acceptance

Acceptance is something that is very difficult for many people. Acceptance is learning to be okay with outcomes, with other people's speech or actions if we can't do anything about it. It makes little sense to stress yourself out or become overwhelmed with emotions when things don't go your way. Whatever one's experience is we must be sure to accept the person as he or she is. This becomes faulty in romantic relationships as well. We need to find acceptance as one is. If you cannot accept a person for who and what they are, then you need to remove yourself. Trying to change another person never works out. We can only change ourselves and our responses.

Judgements

Judgements are wholly an ego thing! Humans place judgement on everything. Who gives us that right? Certainly not soul. Humans place judgement on other humans, the way one might dress or behave or speak. We place judgements on places, situations, events and experiences. We must learn *acceptance* in order not to make judgements. You and I both do not like to be judged so why would you sit in judgement of someone else? It is a purely ego centered thought. Ego sits in judgement of everyone else. It also sits in judgement of you. Tell it to stop. That you've had enough.

Loving Kindness

Now this is something we all must practice. Loving Kindness is a Buddhist way of being in the world. It is about looking into the eyes of another person, be it a family member, a colleague, the person at the checkout line or a complete stranger and know that we are looking into the eyes of Divinity. That person's soul in part of the All That Is, just like us. Loving Kindness is practiced daily in every gesture, speech, action or behavior. It is acceptance of things and people the way they are and showing our love and kindness at all times.

Compassion

Compassion is very close to Loving Kindness. Remember, what goes out from you returns to you. Compassion is the connection we naturally have with other sentient beings. We should feel them. Feel their hardships and suffering and be willing to do something about it, even if it's only comforting someone, causing them to smile, paying a compliment, giving to them something of yourself, and yes, even money. Compassion is the ability for humans to understand another's plight, but also to help alleviate the suffering. Learn to open your heart center and feel compassion.

Empathy

Empathy is similar to Compassion, but different. Empathy is being able to place yourself in the other person's or animal's shoes, so to speak. It is the ability to feel and understand from the others' perspectives. They become our mirror, mirroring back to us our own frailties. Empathy is a necessity toward compassion. Again, open your heart center.

Detachment

Detachment is simply letting go. Humans become attached to people, places and things. When in a relationship we think we feel love, but the relationship is unstable, maybe abusive, maybe controlling, maybe boring. Even if we decide to leave the relationship we still feel a pull. It's difficult to move on. That is attachment. Attachment to things is just as real. These attachments might cause us to become selfish, controlling and greedy. Some humans never want to share even if they have more than enough. These people are hoarders of everything they own. It is also the cause of most misery and strife in our lives. When we are attached to things or people, when they are gone or missing we can actually become neurotic, anxious, distressed, angry, feel a deep sense of loss…over what? We need to learn to practice detachment. If we can let things go, we are free to move on. We become free to do whatever we desire. Detach my friends.

Being intentional is a start toward being your true soul self. It is a pathway to higher consciousness and our divinity. I think I have always practiced love & compassion out in the world even with people I don't know. I can walk down the street with a friend or colleague and I will smile and say hello to others or give a pan handler some money, while my friend will turn up his/her nose in disgust. I laugh and ask why, but the answers are always a transference of my friend's own inner (emotional) stuff. We can't allow what others do to affect how we behave and how we think.

Being intentional with yourself and all you do is a key component of self-discovery. By self I mean your soul self because, that is who you really are, and that is who I really am. I can't drive this home enough. If we all, and I mean all humans, walked through this world as our soul selves, being intentional all the time, we would have no war, famine, disease, illness, struggle, poverty, etc. This does not mean challenges won't find us. Challenges help us grow!

*You can wait and hope and pray that God will deliver you
from the world's evils and pitfalls...OR...you can be
the Child of God and create your own reality, deliver yourself
from the evils and pitfalls, and choose to create joy, prosperity,
abundance and pure love in your life! You have within you
the very talents, gifts and abilities as your maker!
Be a Co-Creator, not a waiter!*
Dr. Sandy Range

CHAPTER NINE

Authenticity

It is of utmost importance to be or become our authentic selves. What is authenticity with the self? It is first knowing who you are. Most people do not know who they are. They think they are their name or what they do for a living. This is not who you are. Your name is simply how the world can identify you. Your job is simply what you do to make a living. People have identified who they are by listing their hobbies, their skills & talents, their clothing, their culture and more. That's not it!

It doesn't matter where you came from, your family of origin, your nationality, your religion, your gender or your age. None of that matters. Who you ARE is soul. A divine being. That's who you are. You will need to recognize and acknowledge this. You will need to incorporate this knowing into your consciousness and your heart center. You cannot be your authentic self unless and until you become your true self: soul.

I went through my own identity crisis in my teens and twenties. It was a very difficult time for me. I remember finally identifying all the different nationalities of my bloodlines, all the varying cultures within the family, the religious and spiritual teachings and being pulled from one set of beliefs to another. I did not know who I was. It took many years and a Native American mentor to help me resolve my dilemma. I chose the indigenous path at that time because it rang true for me. It was a way of life, not a system of beliefs and blind following.

Later in life and after much study and many spiritual teachers and mentors, I realized that I did not have to identify with one particular set of beliefs, values or ideology. I had finally come to the brilliant conclusion that what and who I truly am is simply soul. A magnificent, enlightened, creator soul. A soul connected to the All That Is, to the Universe and all its' creations and manifestations. I and the Universe are ONE! I found my authentic self.

What does it mean to live your life as soul? It means continuing to work on yourself and the planet, ever growing, ever evolving. It means living in the light and not the dark. It means you walk through the world with integrity and honor. It means you are impeccable in everything you do. Impeccability is the soul's integrity. To be impeccable is to be pure, pristine and flawless. If you think this is too difficult just look at the life you are living now without even acknowledging you are soul! I'll bet it's been real difficult. Don't worry about reaching the impeccability bar just yet. Just strive to get there. While we are still in this human form we will always be faced with challenges. In a previous chapter I spoke about challenges and how we will always face them. As a reminder, they help us to grow and evolve. When you engage your life in this work and when those challenges come to present themselves, we are better able to stand up and see through the quagmire, the fog, the disillusionment of the situation and find the answer or solution.

We so very often look outside of ourselves for comfort, emotional nurturing, answers, love, companionship, more sustenance to live our daily lives. We walk through this life with blinders on never seeing the true beauty of this world. The media does us no favors when it comes to seeing what is going on in the world. They make their money by showing us only the darkness. It may not be their fault entirely either. After all, we are the ones pushing up their ratings by wanting to see more destruction, devastation, murders, thefts, corruption, wars – shall I go on? Which of you live for this stuff? This is how you lower your vibratory frequencies, become heavier, denser energetically and more stuck. Stop watching the news. I haven't watched the news for more than a decade. I do tune in at the exact time the weather report comes on, so you can't use that for an excuse. When the weather is over, turn it off! And stay away from the dark streams of social media as well!

You can begin to find your authentic self by going within. That's right, within is where your true self lies. How do you go within? By turning off the phone, the TV, the Laptop, putting your book down, and finding a quiet space where you won't be disturbed. Once in that quiet space sit comfortably, but not laying down or twisted up like a pretzel. Keep your neck and spine straight, but not rigid. Now, take a long slow deep breath through the nose and exhale long and slow through your mouth. Do that about three times. Focus on your breath even while breathing naturally. Focus on the breath will keep all the rooftop chatter away. Just sit in silence with yourself. Start with just a full five minutes. Each day add five minutes until you can sit in silence for up to an hour. More on this in a later chapter.

What happens when you sit in the silence? Many things can happen, but you will need to set your intention. Remember being *intentional* in the previous chapter? The intention you want to set should be one of honesty and truth. Ask the question: Who am I really? Or just say: Show me who I truly am. Sitting in the silence with a strong intention will get you an answer. If you don't get anything right away, keep at it. It takes practice to be still enough to receive answers. Sometimes they come as a magnificent epiphany. Sometimes they come as intuition. Sometimes they come as an inner whisper. Sometimes they come as a visual or a very strong feeling. The answers will come. Just keep at it. And the more you do this the more you will tune in to your soul self in the process. Remember it took me years to find out who I am, but you have help now.

Some of us are hurting so badly we can't see through the pain. All we know is hurt and suffering. Some of us may think about ending this life on planet earth. You could, but you'd only have to come back and repeat it again and again until you get it right. Why not get it right – right now? We spoke about karma earlier. We will come back to pay our karmic debts, but we can also eliminate or minimize past karma by how we choose to live right now today.

Learn to become your authentic self. Learn to tune into your soul knowing, but be careful to discern the difference between what soul is telling you and what ego is telling you. Remember, ego is a trickster and you will need to put ego in its place from time to time. Sometimes you will have watch it every step of the way. After all, ego has had full reign of your life up until now.

We all need to wake up to our authentic selves. I cannot stress the importance of living a life that is strong and true. Some of you may have never known what it is to be authentic. Some of you may have discovered authenticity in spurts and bounds. Some of you may have thought you were being authentic, but it was only ego playing on you. If you have already found your authenticity then teach others to do the same.

In Western society and culture many have come to deny their souls. They live in a plastic bubble of hopeless and endless perpetuity. They have become blind to beauty, to the good people, to the helpers and healers. They think holistic and alternative health is quackery. They believe there is no climate change, no melting polar ice caps, no polluted waterways, no pharmaceutical companies keeping us sick. They go through life negating everything they can't see, feel or touch. The air they breathe is odorless (for the most part), colorless, tasteless and you can't touch it or hold it yet we are breathing it. They know it's there. Some of them have full faith in God, but they've never seen him/her. Would it suffice to say that there are many things in this universe that cannot be held, seen, tasted, smelled, but are very, very real!

To become authentic you'll have to redefine how you see yourself. Remove all the crap holding you down, Remove the excess baggage: Do you carry a steamer trunk or coin purse? Throw off the burdens that don't belong to you. Why hold on to other people's stuff, eh?

Life really is a miracle. My message to you is to be mindful in your everyday life. Once you have mastered your authenticity you will be aware and mindful of those special little gifts that present themselves. If we can get out of our own way and tune in to what spirit guides us to do we cannot go wrong. Be in acceptance and open to receive. Pain, whether mental, emotional or physical, can have a tendency to blind us to the miracles all around us. We just need to wake up to the beauty of life in all its forms. Even those souls who live in a body that is disabled or a body in chronic pain or illness, you have the ability and the leeway to remove negative karma. You have chosen this body and this pain through this lifetime on purpose to help you excel in your learning and remove negative karma. It is not a punishment. It is a gift. A chosen gift.

What people don't realize is that your thoughts can keep you stuck and in pain or they can release everything holding you back including your pain. It all comes down to choice. Choose freedom from pain and struggle. Then act on it. Once you are in the flow of your soul things have a way of manifesting in your life. But…right now, you are still manifesting all the struggle and pain because that's all you think about. What you think about you bring about.

My point is that everyone plays a part in the changes to come. If you are not being your authentic self you will, most likely, be unable to live your life manifesting what your true self needs and wants for you during and after the shift. I cannot reiterate enough how important becoming your authentic self is. Just do it!

> *"Our weaknesses are not our downfall.*
> *They are simply gifts given for our awakening.*
> *They are shown to us so that we may acknowledge and*
> *Understand where and how we need to grow."*
> Dr. Sandy Range

CHAPTER TEN

Meaning Making

What is meaning and how do we find it? We all have so much going on in our daily lives it's often difficult to find our meaning. We work long hours to make ends meet, we have children to attend to and nurture, maybe we are in school studying for an advanced degree. We have shopping and errands to run, going to the gym, preparing for the next day and never getting enough sleep. Even when we find some down time we become absorbed in social media, texting, catching up on emails. It's no wonder we haven't even been able to look up for a moment. One day, however, we do look up and ask, "What does it all mean?" Does my life have meaning? Time slips away and before we know it our 20s, 30s 40s and 50s have passed us by. Wait! What?

The search for meaning is not about our life's accomplishments. It's not about what we've accumulated or how many (or few) goals we've reached. Meaning is about the human soul. It is about what we experience within and how we move through and past suffering. Every human being, when in times of suffering, experiences that suffering individually, mentally, emotionally and at times physically. It appears that our human constitution awakens when suffering is present. We begin to look within and ask how did I get here? What did I do wrong?

The soul emerges and the spirit awakens. Meaning becomes a process of the spiritual self: that higher consciousness we all possess. It is our individual duty to recognize and realize that we are more than a brain and a body living as robots according to our daily needs and demands. To find meaning we all must turn within and seek the connection to our higher selves. We do not have to wait until we are 50 or 60 or 80 years of age. We can do it now.

There are many advantages to connecting with our own spirit selves. The spirit or higher consciousness or divine spirit is ours by birth right, yet we ignore its existence and therefore lose out on its guidance and knowledge. Meaning gets lost. In the silence is where we hear the subtle voice of inspiration, guidance and knowing. It takes practice to hear that soft voice and there are varying avenues to help us reach that state of awareness. Meditation is the best way, but there is also prayer, devotion and mindfulness. In meditation we sit in stillness with devotion to our Creator. Meditation is different from prayer in that in prayer we are giving thanks, and asking for blessings (which is just fine). In meditation we sit in silence and here is where we hear our Creator speak to us through our higher consciousness. However, we must be careful to differentiate between the ego mind and the higher consciousness. The ego mind is always vying for attention and will tell us what it thinks we want to hear.

We no longer have to be in crisis or suffering to awaken to our birth right. Meaning becomes evident to knowledge of greater things that can lead our lives into greater awareness, better decision making and soulful fulfillment.

In order to understand Meaning Making we need to know that there are no accidents and no coincidences in life. Everything happens for a reason. EVERYTHING! It is up to us to figure out why bad things keep happening and why good things keep happening and why things stay the same. If we use our hindsight we are able to look back and see what it was that caused a thing to happen whether good or bad. And don't forget that there is a lesson in everything.

When we can look back and gain insight into a thing we can then make meaning of it, especially when we have discovered the lesson it provided to us.

I remember a few years ago when my leg hurt so badly I almost couldn't walk. The doctors told me I had spinal stenosis and sciatica that went all the way from my lower back down my right leg into my lower calf. The pain was unbearable and kept me from my workouts, from walking, from riding the beautiful horses I love so much. It kept me from everything. I still managed my practice, but I was in constant and persistent pain. I finally had surgery to correct the issue. That took another seven months to recover from. My dilemma was why did this happen at such a crucial time in my life? I was building my practice and adding new services. I was looking for a bigger place to accommodate new clients and services. What I was made to understand was that I had been internalizing my lack of help from family and friends and everywhere else.

Issues with the spine have to do with support. The spine does support our whole body so when it goes out of whack be aware if you have any support or a support system in your life. Even if you don't you'll need to be conscious of any emotions you may be harboring. What I did when I finally realized my why is that I needed to acknowledge and understand what I was harboring or internalizing and let it go. I was still able to continue working on my project.

I was able to make meaning out of my temporary disability. We need to learn to *make meaning* of the things that happen in our lives. Every illness or accident happens for a reason. It may appear to be extreme, but then, sometimes we need extreme measures to wake us up! Even the good things that happen need Meaning Making. If you are one of the so-called "lucky ones'," why? What is the reason you won that lottery ticket or got that promotion or found the perfect partner? If you don't understand the reason you won't understand yourself or your growth. In understanding the why we are able to expunge negative emotions that we may not have realized we had, including ego!

Meaning Making for our lives is a process of using our innate abilities to see better, clearer and further. By that I mean we are able to see within, to see the real, to see what we usually hide even from ourselves. There are many things we hide from ourselves. All of us have done wrong or did something inherently bad or that we just weren't proud of at some point (or more) in our lives. We need to look at them all. When we have looked with better eyes, we will see what we have done and then we are able to correct it and begin balancing our karma and clearing our path.

See everything you have done. Feel it as though you are doing it again. Look at the person or animal or whatever, whether in your mind or in the room, then from deep within your heart and soul, ask for forgiveness and really mean it. You may become emotional, you may cry, you may even become angry through this process. That is a good thing unless you can't let it go.

We need to ask forgiveness for all the wrongs we have done in our lives. This true and deep forgiveness allows you to free the person and free yourself, but again, it must be true and heart felt. What this does is remove negative karma. It helps to free you up so you can do the deeper work that needs to be done.

What is also important is to NOT place blame. Placing blame is a judgement. It further induces a weight so heavy that you won't be able to get out from under it. When we place blame we are side stepping our own part in a thing. We must learn to recognize and acknowledge our part in things and to take ownership. Ownership is a giant step forward

We begin to purge all the old, outdated, useless behaviors, thoughts and speech. This may mean developing your inner sight to see things with better eyes, develop your inner ears to listen with better hearing and accuracy and develop your speech to communicate with a better and more loving heart. Out with the old. In with the new! You will have to re-design yourself from the inside out. Not the outside in. Spirit doesn't care about fashion, makeup, what kind of car you drive, or what kind of house you live in. When it comes right down to it, none of that matters. What matters is getting your soul right!

Most people believe they don't have the power to change themselves never mind the world and its indifference and lack of interest, plain and simple. There are delusional human beings on this planet of two kinds: they have either delusions of grandeur or delusions of insignificance. We have all known people who have delusions of grandeur. They boast, come on strong, they think they are the center of the universe. This is ego playing you! Then there is the delusion of insignificance. This is the person who plays low key. This person has low self-esteem, may lack confidence, and does not believe in him/herself. Stays in the shadows of life and makes themselves small. The lesson here is to decide which delusion you are currently walking through the world in?

Learn to make meaning of your life as a whole. Meaning Making for your life means having a purposeful life. A life full with meaning. If you already are living a purposeful, meaningful life, then take it to the next level. If you have not yet found your meaning or purpose this book will help you do that!

*"Why do people fear so much? Fear runs the lives of too many.
A life based in fear produces misery for the person
and everyone around them.
Your thoughts become things... Shift your perspective.
You can choose what you want to think and
what you think you create in your reality!"*
Dr. Sandy Range

CHAPTER ELEVEN

Your Mental and Physical Wellness

In past chapters we've seen a repeating theme: "what you think about you bring about." Have you ever wondered why so many people across the globe, and especially in this USA, suffer from debilitating illness mentally, emotionally, and physically? Have you made any connections as to the causes? Yes, there is more than one cause and while your thoughts do play a big part in your overall health and wellness, there are some other causes we need to look at. We'll come back to our mental wellness in a bit! Please don't be frightened by what you will read below. This is information to inform and enlighten you.

Oh No! GMO!

There are a myriad number of assaults on our bodies every single day. Even if you live in a city, suburb, or the country you are bombarded by air born pesticides from local crops and the foods we purchase at the grocery store. Pollution gets into our skin, hair, lungs from manufacturing and industrial plants, automobiles, fossil fuels (oil and coal refineries). It even pollutes us through our wood burning stoves. Not only that, but we are willfully polluting ourselves from the skin products, hair products, soaps, perfumes, nail polish – and ladies, please stop getting those gel nails! It's all poison and toxic. One more thing about crops, most crops being grown by factory farmers and even some local farmers are Genetically Modified Organism (GMO) crops. If you don't know what they are or you don't believe it's true, you had better get started on your own research. GMO's and GEOs (Genetically Engineered Organisms) are real.

These GMOs and Ges are created by the biggest maker of GMO & GE crops and seeds in the US this particular company is also the maker of the biggest brand of weed killer: Round Up. Tell me why a pesticide company is in the food business. The two just don't mix! This company and others have a big stake in the food we eat, the clothes we wear, the products we put on our bodies. When you think about it the biggest GMO crops are corn, wheat and soy. These products are in nearly everything we eat. Everything!

Meat eaters, you are not in the clear. The GMO grains (corn & wheat) are what your cows, chickens, pigs, goats and other factory farm produced animals eat. It is their feed pure and simple. Not to mention the horrific circumstances of these animals' living conditions, inhumane treatment and disgusting slaughter practices. So, not only are you ingesting GMO laden meats, dairy & eggs, you are ingesting the fear hormones and toxins produced in the flesh of these animals along with growth hormones, antibiotics, the countless vaccines and medications given to these animals all too often. Did you know that these GMO seeds are what factory farmers are forced to grow? As well, GE crops are able to withstand the Round Up pesticides sprayed on them. You are eating this stuff! I watched a documentary where a GMO crop of corn was videotaped as an insect, a grasshopper, took two tiny bites from a leaf on the stalk. The insect immediately fell off the stalk. And within seconds its' gut exploded. You are eating this crap! What is it doing to you and your children?

So, everything you buy at the grocery store to consume most likely has GMO grains or ingredients. If you buy cereal, snacks, or any pre-packaged foods you are eating GMOs. These toxic foods cause a great many illnesses, along with obesity, that researchers and physicians are now attempting to get out to the public. The information is available to you. Be proactive and do your own research.

The wholesome foods of the past. The foods you grandmother and great grandmother prepared had no GMOs. They were healthy farm raised foods at that time because there were no poisons being fed into the food stream. People were a lot healthier then as well! I do what I can to grow my own organic foods and herbs. You can too! Nutrition has a great deal to do with your mental health and wellbeing. The foods and nutrients we put into our bodies can heal us or make and keep us ill.

Sometimes I wonder if it's only the USA that is behind the eight ball? Most other *so-called* first world countries have banned GMO seeds and crops, use alternative treatments and remedies for our health and are ramping up alternative sources of power like solar, wind and thermal. We can each do our part in reversing climate change by being mindful of your use of plastics and other non-recyclable materials. Use reusable shopping bags, don't use plastic straws or cups, stop eating from fast food restaurants, and do you really need to by expensive designer clothing? If you don't own a home or are struggling to pay your rent you don't need designer clothes, nails, hair or anything else! If you think the climate, pollution and toxic poisons aren't affecting you, think again!

The medications you take might be keeping you ill. If you take more than one or two medications and if you are taking any medications on a long term basis they are keeping you ill. If you have found that you experience side effects from prescribed medications and tell your doctor, he or she will prescribe another medication to counteract the side effects or one that is stronger and deadlier for your long term health problem.

Be mindful that doctors are not like they used to be. They are trained now to follow a certain protocol. They no longer establish a patient/doctor relationship with you. They sit at a computer and ask you scheduled questions about your health. Many of your concerns may not be addressed as the insurance companies may not provide benefits to addressing a specific illness or concern. They just won't pay for it!

Doctors in medical school are trained and mandated to follow the pharmaceutical companies' recommendations for ==providing symptom alleviation – NOT cures! No medication on the market can cure an illness==. They simply cover up the symptoms. When you have a back ache you take an aspirin or an NSAID to relieve the pain. I made that mistake myself when I went through my Spinal Stenosis and Sciatic pain. I kept taking Naproxen to reduce the pain to the point that I had no idea how damaged my spine really was. It didn't cure me. It hid the problem from me. Doctors in hospitals and clinics are not even allowed to speak with you about medical cannabis that has miraculous properties in healing and alleviating and ending symptoms of Parkinson's disease, ADHD, Autism, seizures, even Cancer! They're not even allowed to speak about or recommend alternative treatments.

Now, I'm not telling you to stop taking your medications. I am, however, asking you to speak with your doctor about natural alternatives. She or he may not be able to provide you much help in that area since they are handcuffed to the pharmaceutical industry. I would suggest, if you can afford one, to see a Naturopathic or Homeopathic physician. You can also start researching which natural remedies may do a better job at healing you than the medications you're already taking. Don't forget eating organic foods as well.

Your Mental Health

All of these things plays an imperative role in your mental & physical health. There are so many mental illnesses like Depression, Anxiety, ADHD, PTSD, Mania, Bipolar Disorder, and even some organic mental disorders like Schizophrenia, can be alleviated and healed with good nutrition and holistic alternatives that may include herbal medicines & supplements, plant medicines, essential oils, medical cannabis and more.

So now, getting back to our thoughts – ==changing the way you think about and process information can open your mind to the Universe!== Yes, I said it! What you think about manifests itself in your immediate world. If you think doom and gloom that's what you get. If you think light and love that's what you get. As an example, I had a patient for over 3 years who just couldn't get out of his own way. It didn't matter that he was provided all the tools and strategies to help him change his thinking about himself and his family issues. I would press him and then allow him time to process the information and put it to use. It was very difficult for him to allow himself to forgive himself. I was beginning to think that this may be the one client I can't help.

One day he came to my office and said, "I think I get it now." His frumpy frowning face was now lit with light and enthusiasm. He was a completely different person. For the next 4 months my client utilized every single tool I had given him over the previous three years. He became more outgoing, more social and much happier with his life. Even though his family situation remained the same, he was able to change his thoughts and his perspective and see things differently. He realized that he was not to blame and neither was his mother. Life is just life.

Another client of mine, a meditation class client, loved the guided meditation practice, but could not incorporate the lessons from the classes. She always said, "I get it intellectually, but not spiritually. I know all there is to know, but I'm not very good at implementing it in my life." Now, I've known many people, including myself at one point, that are able to learn things intellectually and academically, but have a hard time applying it in practical ways. The only way to really get it, to fully understand it, is to do the hard work.

My client was made aware of the blocks in front of her. These blocks were her programming from childhood. She grew up a staunch Christian and, according to her, meditation was feared as some sort of devil work. Once she realized what was holding her back she simply made the choice to hold these earlier learnings as false teachings that she no longer needed to hold on to. It took a little while, but my client eventually was able to move forward in her meditation practice to where she could sit alone in meditation for about 45 minutes every morning. This made a huge difference in her relationships, social life, work life and family life.

Yes, sometimes we need a little help to get out of our own way and that's okay. If you think you need a little help, make the choice to find a therapist or counselor with a background in holistic or spiritual counseling to help you. It could make all the difference in the world. A therapist is an objective person who will listen to you intently. He or she will also provide insights and helpful suggestions to help you heal what needs healing.

We really need to wake ourselves up and stop sleepwalking through life. The information you need is out there. Read books and articles, find a documentary, YouTube, Google the information, but just make sure it's credible. Stop watching the news. You won't get the factual information you need from that media! (See *Resources* at the end of this book.)

Now that you're getting your mind and body healed and whole, or at least removing the toxins and want to stay that way you can begin to work on your soul self! Do you realize that everything is connected? Just like your body's connective tissues keep us from literally falling apart, every organ plays a role in keeping us strong, healthy and able to live to a ripe old age. Stop poisoning your brain, blood and organs and do what you can to avoid outside sources of toxins.

But they're so creepy! I'm afraid!

We are all connected, one to the other. There is no me without you and no you without me. We are also connected to every sentient being in the Universe and especially on this planet. Yes, you are one with the worm, the cricket and the cockroach. You are connected with the trees and plants (the tree people), the rocks (stone people), the flying ones, the swimming ones and the creeping ones, along with all two-leggeds and 4-leggeds. So, when you swat that fly or step on that ant you are murdering one of your relatives.

We need to allow the fear that makes us afraid of these creatures and other humans to transform. Fear is at the root of all ignorance, anger and violence. Fear is what makes people (the 2-leggeds) go into flight, fight or freeze mode. But why are we afraid? We are afraid because we lack understanding of who we really are. When you recognize your soul self, you allow the transformation from fear to gnosis begin. Wouldn't it be great to never be afraid again? Ego's job is to keep you safe. Once ego is put in check and allowed to only do its' job then you have nothing to worry about.

Now I'm not saying that no difficulties, accidents or illness will befall you (karma). I am saying that at the root of all our difficulties is fear. So when we can release fear and embrace what is, we have a better chance at changing our condition. Our thoughts have everything to do with how we are present in the world. There are many people out there who are just plain fear mongers. They thrive (ego) on making others afraid. Our government is doing just that. It is passing laws and instigating fear in the masses. In turn the masses create havoc. Just recently 12 suspicious packages were sent to various

political figures of a certain party and 12 senior citizens were gunned down in a synagogue. We see it over and over all over this country and the world. What is the reason? Intimidation? Why? Because people are afraid. No, I still don't watch the news, but I hear about it from everyone around me. The above mentioned references I did look up so I could be accurate in my reporting.

When people are afraid they become something else. They intimidate because this is how they can feel more powerful. Fear causes more harm, accidents, and illness than any other emotion. We cause our own harm, our own difficulties, our own struggles and strife by how we think and perceive the world around us. We can see the world as full of scary things to hide from or avoid, or we can see the world as inherently good. Remember, what you think about you bring about. So how about shifting your perception and seeing the world as a thing of beauty.

"I will see you again. If you need a hand that's what I'm here for.
To help you get there!
Honor your ancestors. They are you in spirit.
The ancestors are with us always.
They are our strength.
They ask for us to remember them."
Dr. Sandy Range

CHAPTER TWELVE

The Ancestors

Our ancestors are a very important part of ourselves and our humanity. One day you and I will become ancestors, but until then know that they look to us to remember them, to honor them, to communicate with them. All knowledge lies in our roots...our blood...our connections to the Creation. Go deep! Know thyself through your ancestors.

It doesn't matter what nationality you are or where you come from or even the color of your skin. We all come from tribal peoples. Do you know what tribe(s) you are from? If you do bravo! If not, try taking a DNA test to see where your ancestors originated. That is a road you'll travel with curiosity and wonder!

The ancestor story begins with us. If you are a young person then you have a lot of work to do. If you are an elder person, you have a lot of work to do. This just means both young and old need to become aware of our own stories and how they will be told when we are gone. What truths about our origins, cultures, nationalities, and societies will we reveal? What magic is deep within the roots of our being that we would uncover? The ancestor story is a fascinating, powerful and intimate dance with those who've come before us and laid out our path.

The young ones believe they have enough time to get their acts together, but this isn't true. The time is now, no matter how young you are. Moms, grand moms and caretakers teach your children to grow into wise and learned elders. What the young learn now will propel them into the realm of light and spirit. The young people appear to be carefree and living however they choose, but we know better. The young people today are smart, capable of amazing feats, more knowledgeable about the workings of the world than in many generations before them. They are wiser. They know what's wrong with the world and some of them have brilliant ideas to make it right.

It's important for us to nurture these young people and their ideas. It's important for us to stop and listen to them without cutting them off or demeaning them in some way, intentionally or not. It's important for us to bring young people together to share their view of the world and dream it into being. We must support our young people to live lives that will make a difference. They are our future. How will the world or even our society change if we do not create, nurture and maintain the change makers?

Elders, your time is now. Do the work that must be done to relieve yourself of any old and outdated mental and emotional burdens. Do you have any regrets about your life or regrets about those you have known? Begin now to clear away those regrets. Settle any relationship issues you may have had with relatives or friends. Even if you are asking for forgiveness of those who are no longer here, ask still. Know you are forgiven and forgive yourself. Regrets having to do with never accomplishing or completing something are not regrets really. They are dreams that you never worked on and that's okay. You are where you are meant to be in this time and space. It is all divine order. That is the lesson.

Elders are very special people. No matter how long or short you have been on this earth you have gained knowledge, insight, and wisdom in some manner. Many of you have already done your work and are happy and content in your lives. For many others, you are still struggling. You want to be free of the burdens and try very hard to make change. For both of you, you know how this world works because you have lived it for many, many decades, seeing presidents come and go, and feeling the rights and wrongs of our society. You have seen both beauty and atrocities and you have been resilient through it all.

Your life is a miracle and don't ever let anyone tell you any different. You are the miracle. You are Creator's gift to the world. It doesn't matter if you never became that big bank president or the CEO of that other company. It doesn't matter if you are a waitress in a diner or the maintenance man at the local elementary school. You are a miracle because you have given of yourself in miraculous ways to serve and to bless whether you know that or not.

If you are an elder begin thinking about your life and relationships. If someone has wronged you forgive him or her. This is for you more than anyone else. Talk to your children and grandchildren. Tell them about you and your life story and the stories of family members that are no longer here. Give them something to hold on to that is rich and satisfying.

Even the stories of slavery and internment should be told so your children know what your family has withstood and come through. You are here after all. You are living proof of that cord of ancestral strength and power. Give them a taste of that strength, they will relish in it. However, let them know they don't have to be ashamed of any of it. All of that history is what makes you and your family precious and unique. It's all in the blood! If there are stories of triumph and success, let them know! Even those stories about great auntie Cheli who was a medicine woman, shaman, or healer. Now, that is a strong ancestral and tribal connection.

Now, let me explain a little about ancestral bloodlines. We think of our ancestors as all those relatives who were older than us and who have transitioned. However, we all have ancestors that may not be in our bloodlines. They could have been a non-familial caretaker after one's parents passed away. They could be people who were very close and loving like a close family friend. They can even be people who have helped us along the way as a mentor who coached us through our first job or a person we study under in order to become as good as they are or better. Ancestors can also be a younger sibling, cousin or other young relative who transitioned from this earth before us.

We have tens of thousands of ancestors. In doing ancestral work we want to call on those ancestors that are healed and whole. This means they have been gone from us for quite some time. We may not even know who they are. The more recently transitioned ancestors are still healing and may have issues to work out on the other side. This is why we call upon the old ones, the ancient ones. They are full with wisdom. We call upon them to assist in the healing of our most recently transitioned and then we can ask them to help to heal our living generation. We are their descendants. We are their family. They await our asking of them to help us.

Now, if you haven't already, make a connection with your ancestors. Go to visit them if you know where they lie. If you do not know where they lie find photos or ask family members for information about them. However, do not mourn or grieve, especially for the more recent ancestors. When we grieve them for too long we hold them here in this realm of existence and they cannot make the full transition to become healed and whole again in spirit. Many times they remain because they are concerned about our well-being. It could be considered selfish if we don't allow our loved ones to transition fully. I'm not telling you not to mourn, just grieve in a healthy way and know you must release your loved one. After all, we want to and should be able to transition fully. Once transitioned and healed, we can always come back to visit our loved ones if we are asked.

In the USA November is Native American Heritage month. For me, I celebrate it all year round. Come Thanksgiving week, I am pulled by the beat of a different drum, a Native drum. You see, my birthday falls on Thanksgiving Day every 4 years or so (both joy and sadness). This day, along with Columbus Day in October I do not celebrate. I will be quite happy when this entire country is Columbus Day FREE! Celebrating would be like having a party at the genocide of my own people. T-Day week is our "Days of Mourning" with lots of prayers, singing, Talking Circles (to process the trauma), comfort, support, kindness, compassion, giveaways, sweat lodges and some fasting. We usually end the week with celebration in honor of our ancestors and the fact that we are still here, alive and strong all over this Nation. We feast, celebrate, and enjoy our relatives and friends, and yes, we do give thanks to our Creator, the Great Spirit for our very being, for being provided for. If you'd like to know more about the true story of Thanksgiving you can read it here: www.manataka.org/page269.html

Among Indigenous tribes, of special importance is the honoring of our ancestors. Our ancestors, we believe, are always with us, guiding us, teaching us, if we listen and see! We honor their lives and their spirits. Our strength is in their numbers on the other side and our elders who pass on cultural traditions. So is our loss if we do not remember them or bother to learn from them.

Honoring our ancestors is honoring ourselves as a people. So too, is the honoring of the ancestors of African Americans and their slave ancestors in this country, and the rich history of their ancestors in Africa. The Japanese Americans (and I'm sure some other Asians as well) who also were put on reservations better known as Internment Camps during WWII. America has a rich history of the genocide of people with a lot more melanin. All over the world there are oppressed peoples with rich and amazing histories and ancestors.

Remember to give thanks for your ability and willingness to honor the rich and diverse histories and cultures of People of Color in this Nation. Indigenous Peoples, African peoples, Asian Peoples, Latinx Peoples all built this Nation through their blood sweat and tears, and many times their very lives, literally! And please know that these comments are not to offend anyone, but to enlighten and hopefully open minds to see clearly the plight of people of color in this Nation and around the world. Diversity is always a blessings if we can ever learn to embrace it!

The diversity of human beings is natural. It is the way we are all meant to be. Each person from the blackest black to the whitest white and all the beautiful shades in between are the way nature made us. Not one is better in any way than the other. Yes, we know about those who colonized Indigenous lands and cultures around the world with their guns and bibles, but today, in the present time we are changing that mindset. People around the globe are standing up and speaking out against people's civil liberties and human rights being trampled upon. Times are changing and we all need to get on the bandwagon less we be left behind.

A lesson imperative for us at this time in the world is that hundreds of thousands of people around the world and right here in the USA are returning to their roots. People are returning to their ancestral ways, the ways of their tribes. For those who do not know who their tribes are, they learn from those who resonate with their own soul. Much of the good medicine that our ancestors used came from the internal space, the center of self and the divine. It comes from the connection we make with Spirit and our ancestors.

People are becoming, once again, a collective society where everyone cares for everyone else. The energy that is being emitted is strong and powerful. And each of you can tap into it. Talk to your ancestors, talk to your elders. Make the connections you need to make!

*You can wait and hope and pray that
God will deliver you from the
world's evils and pitfalls...OR...you can
be the Child of God and create
your own reality, deliver yourself from the evils and
pitfalls, and choose to create joy, prosperity, abundance
and pure love in your life! You have within you the
very talents, gifts and abilities as your maker!
Be a Co-Creator, not a waiter!
Dr. Sandy Range*

PART TWO

FINDING YOUR SOUL AFTER YOU LOSE YOUR MIND!

"Sometimes we must just be still. No music, no TV, no chatter. Being still allows us to tune into that small voice inside and the big voice from the Universe. Be still and listen. You will find the answer, know the solution, make the best decision."
Dr. Sandy Range

CHAPTER THIRTEEN

(C1) How Do I Find My Soul?

So now that you've had the chance to read these words and hopefully you've incorporated the ideology, philosophy and truth within, you are now ready to begin practicing. The following practices will relate to each of the previous chapters and there will be stories about myself and some of my patients, clients and friends to help you see how things work.

In Chapter One we spoke about what the goal is. The goal is to help you purge the energetic density of your physical being and re-align with your true self, to become, once again, connected as One with Divine mind. In order to evolve to this state of Being we need to purge all that is no longer useful to us, emotionally, mentally and physically.

What is especially important in this process is the "lose your mind" part. You will need to lose your mind in order to find your soul. Simply put. Your mind is in the way of connecting to your true self. It does not mean you need to go crazy. After all, the brain mind attached to ego is already a little crazy, right? So, yes, please, lose your ego-mind!

Sitting in the Silence

The first, most important ritual you should perform every single day is *sitting in the silence*. Sitting in the silence opens you up to all the rooftop chatter in your head, ha ha ha! Not so silent up there eh? It can be. Sitting in the silence is the same as sitting down to meditate. Meditation is the root of the practice of finding your true self and living as a soul.

Sanctuary/Sacred Space

Until you're able to perform these practices in your everyday waking life you must first, be sure to set up your sanctuary. This can be a small area in your bedroom or another room in your home where you will most likely not be disturbed when you need to be there. All you need is a small table where you can place objects that are beautiful to you. Cover it with a small pretty cloth or scarf. You may want to include a plant (something living), a picture and/or statue or any object you have an affinity with that brings you joy and pleasure and sets your inner sights toward the spiritual. You also will need a candle. Make sure your candle is in a glass container so you are safe while observing its flame. Either a votive candle or a pillar candle will do. Just make sure it is enclosed for safety. You don't want it to accidentally get knocked over!

Make this area of your room very special. Again, you don't need a lot, but if you have an extra room in your home that you can designate as your sanctuary room, all the better, This way you can decorate it how would like. Think of a temple, church or chapel. Maybe you can sample some aromatherapy, essential oils or incense to burn to create ambience in your sacred space. You will want a meditation cushion or pillow to sit on or even a straight backed chair because you will need to sit in front of your sacred altar. Maybe decorate with sheer and colorful draperies of purple, lavender, pink, blue or any colors that are pleasing to you. If you can listen to peaceful instrumental music like any meditation music, singing bowls even just drumming this will assist in your deepening practice.

Just remember to make this special space sacred and beautiful. The scents, sounds and lighting should always be soft and spiritually enhancing and fulfilling. Sanctuary is a way to retreat from the world and go to your spiritual place. It is your very special and sacred space designed for your spiritual work. Once you are able to perform these practices on autopilot you will still want (not need) your sacred space as a retreat. We'll discuss other meditation practices that you can do outdoors later.

Here is a simple practice for sitting in the silence: Begin this practice right away. This should be the first practice you learn and perfect. Each morning right after you wake sit on the edge of your bed or prop yourself up on your pillows. Do not lay down or you will fall back to sleep. If you have set up your sacred space go there.

- Light your candle and incense.
- Get your music playing (if needed).
- Sit down. You want your spine straight (erect), but comfortable, not rigid. Your Qi or life force needs to move effortlessly through your body via your spinal column.
- Look into your candle's flame.
- Sit in the silence.

Breath Work

To begin the practice of sitting in the silence or meditation you will need to learn to breathe correctly. As humans we go about our days breathing very shallow. Our organs and brain suffer from a lack of oxygen. Proper breath work can also alleviate physical pain and distress among many other ailments. So, let's begin:

> - Sit with spine erect, but comfortable (you can also stand).
>
> - Place your hands on your abdomen/diaphragm (in order to feel your breath).
>
> - Empty your lungs and take a long, slow, deep breath through your nose with mouth closed. Fill lungs to capacity.
>
> - As you inhale visualize peace and the universal light entering your entire body through the top of your head.
>
> - Exhale very slowly through your mouth until your lungs are completely empty. Visualize all toxins, tension and stress being removed through your heart center. Relaxing you completely.
>
> - Repeat the inhalation and exhalation two more times with the visualizations.
>
> - Breathe normally. (Please do not perform the above breathing exercise while walking, driving or working with machinery. You may get lightheaded or dizzy.

Now, look into your candle's flame and just sit for a minimum of 10 minutes. You can set a timer if you'd like or just see how long you can be in the silence. If you find the rooftop chatter is getting in the way return your focus (mindfulness) to your breath. Be mindful of what your breath feels like as it enters your nostrils and fills your lungs. What sensations do you notice? What does your abdomen feel like as the air goes in and then out?

You can also become more mindful of your candle flame. Look into the flame deeply. Notice its colors, the way it moves, the aura of heat that surrounds it. Paying attention to your breath and the candle flame will help keep those random thoughts from taking over your mind. Again, practice makes perfect. Don't worry if the thoughts keep taking over. It does take practice to be able to hold your mind still. Just know that the most learned monks in the Himalayan Mountains also have rooftop chatter. They call it "Monkey Mind."

A Change is Gonna Come

With practice there comes a time on our spiritual paths when we step into another realm of being. The change that takes place feels weird and alien. It does so because the spiritual work we do on this plane of existence is felt in many other planes of existence. The Universe takes notice and change happens.

As we learn to release, as we learn to give, as we learn to love openly we are suddenly thrust into a different state of mind and being. At some point we can feel alone, separate and at the same time connected to everything in the universe. Our friends and family don't understand us anymore. Because of this we think that maybe we are going a little crazy and think about returning to our old selves again. Do *not* do it! *You* are not going crazy. You got rid of that remember? You are living as a soul now. That is the purpose!

This change, this transformation is the next step in our growth and evolution. As we grow spiritually, mindful of every thought and deed, mindful of our speech and our behavior, we become something else. We become something more. Our energy is more vibrant. Our frequencies vibrate higher and faster. We become the Light in the world.

Please do not be frightened of this new way of being. You will lose what you have gained. Instead, turn up the volume of your spirit filled energy and move through the world as spirit would. We all are spirit after all.

Don't worry about family and friends. Sometimes we make the mistake of lowering our vibrations to meet those of the people around us. Instead raise your vibrations and soon those people around you will elevate as well depending on their individual karma.

We are divine beings with a mission on this earth. If you are still struggling with your spirituality seek out an enlightened teacher or holistic therapist to help you. The world itself is changing. You see the upheaval every day. There are powers at work making way for a much bigger change. We are part of that change. YOU are part of that change. It's all about love and evolution!

So now, make it a point to sit in the silence every single day. It's best to sit in the early morning after you rise to set the intention for your day. If you're unable to sit in the morning then you can sit in the silence at night or even during the day if you are at home and the kids are at school or work. Go ahead and sit in sanctuary. However you need to get it done is fine as long as you get it done.

*Oneness is a concept that we all need to realize and incorporate with every breath we take.
We are all One. We affect everything and everyone else around us.
Each person we touch, in a good way or a bad way, affects all the people they touch and on and on.
Be mindful of your oneness with all and act accordingly.*
Dr. Sandy Range

CHAPTER FOURTEEN

(C2) About Being Mindful and How!

Earlier, chapter two reported that mindfulness is simply being present. How many times do we go about our day, maybe while at work, and someone is talking to us? We hear what the person is saying, but we already have an answer waiting before they even finish. It may be a friend who needs a listening ear, but we, instead, don't listen and offer our advice because we think we know how to solve the problem for our friend. The point is, we are NOT listening and we are barely hearing. If you have an answer ready before a person has finished speaking ego is getting in the way.

We must learn to be mindful in all we do. It is the one thing that keeps us in the present. When we are living in the past through our memories or predicting the future through our imaginings, we are not living fully in the present. Thinking we can predict or imagine a future outcome or if we're always bringing up or referring to the past, keeps us stuck there. How much of our lives do we waste in the past or the future? Way too much. We lose out on so much in the present. Think about it this way –

I had a patient who lived perpetually in the past. He was burdened by things he had done when he was a teenager and young adult. Now in his fifties he just could not release the past. No matter what I offered to this patient to help him move into the present was lost on him. He set up his sanctuary in his bedroom, but felt he needed to meditation to You Tube videos. I didn't see this as a problem until he told me how he ends up perusing alien and supernatural videos for hours at a time and by the time he would sit down in the silence he had too many images in his mind to actually be mindful in the present. In fact he would become overwhelmed by the images and thoughts his You Tube watching would produce.

My patient was provided insight into mindfulness and his sacred space. He was asked to forego watching You Tube and to take a walk in nature instead. He was also asked to be mindful of his emotional states while taking that walk. He was asked to observe what he was seeing, smelling, hearing, witnessing all around him and to incorporate those feelings within himself. He was then asked to conjure feelings of love and acceptance if he hadn't already done so.

It took about 5-6 weeks of performing this same task on a daily basis for my patient to finally be able to sit in the silence and just be with himself – full with feelings of love.

Love is the one emotion that we need to incorporate in our daily lives. Every person we see each day, whether a stranger at the store, a family member, a friend or co-worker is a Soul. All humans are souls experiencing a human life. We need to see them all as Divine Beings even when they don't act like it. Think on this: If you made a series of bad mistakes would you want people to see you as an awful human being or as a divine being living a human existence with all the frailties of human life?

Being mindful in the moment will allow us to become witnesses to the truth of the world. That truth is not all bad! In fact, for the most part it is inherently good. The more people wake up to their soul truth, the more people will create positive change in the world. Are you one of those people? I truly hope so!

To Be Mindful:

- ➤ Practice sitting in the silence. This will help you to know how mindfulness works (see previous chapter).

- ➤ Stay in the Present Moment. This is the precursor to being mindful. One cannot be mindful if dwelling in the past or the future. Remember, the only reality is in the present moment. The future has not happened and the past is already gone. Neither one exists in the present moment.

- ➤ As you shower and dress in the mornings (or whenever) be mindful of every move you make while bathing. What does the soap feel like over your body or the water running over your skin? What does it feel like while drying off and putting on your clothes one item at a time, etc? Slow down. Be mindful.

- ➤ As you walk to the bus stop or to your car be mindful of your steps and how you are moving very deliberately. Are you moving across dirt or grass or pavement? How does that feel under your feet? How do you move differently across each one?

- ➤ When eating a meal, sit down and pay attention to every mouthful. Chew your food slowly. What does the food feel like in your mouth? What does it taste like? How does it feel sliding down your throat and entering your belly? You will also know when you are full sooner through this technique.

- ➤ Practice mindful listening with others. Do you really hear what the person is saying or are you already formulating a response while he or she is still speaking?

> Mindful speaking. Be careful of your words. Your words have the power to heal or to harm. Once they have left your mouth you cannot take them back. Take a breath before you respond to someone and formulate your words carefully being mindful of each word and its intention.

> Be Mindful in everything you do each and every day. This will allow you to become more aware and awake and lead you to your higher consciousness.

> Being mindful always opens you up to receiving. You become more aware of when spirit or the Universe is blessing you through the ways this world works. That means a blessings could come by way of a person, a situation or circumstance or any means at all!

> These will help you. Go to: https://www.mindfulnesscds.com/ and choose a Mindfulness CD or DVD from Jon Kabot-Zinn, the leading expert on Mindfulness.

I've often asked myself what is it we fear when it comes to one individual accepting self as one with every other individual and nature herself upon this earth. We all want world peace, love and oneness, but we can't seem to let go of our own personal desires and fears. Many people think they will not make a difference in the larger scheme of things. "I'm too small to have an impact," they say. No one is too small and no one is insignificant. Each time you take the high road, each time you share kindness, each time you recycle, each time you help someone, you are making a difference. We've all heard of "paying it forward," Don't just pay it forward…show and tell! Let others see your kind and conscious works. We must take the lead and lead by example, but leave ego out of it.

Being mindful in your everyday life will cause you to become aware and awake in everything you do. It will allow you to actually see others for who they really are. It will allow you to go beyond the superficial and delve deep into the *real* of humanity and our planet.

==Once you have mastered mindfulness you can master yourself by understanding your own thoughts and insights, and understanding and controlling ego.== We definitely want to control ego.

Be brave! Go out into your world and explore via mindfulness. You will see, hear, feel, taste and smell so much more of your world, and be all the wiser and clearer for it!

Speaking of change.

Lessons Learned and Appreciated! I want to talk to you about my Spiritual surgery (oops! I mean) Spinal Fusion surgery. I am still in a recovery mode even as I write these words. Initially it was very difficult. I couldn't walk or sit up without assistance. I had no appetite and lost a very welcomed 17 pounds. I pondered why this happened and why the pain was so very severe, literally incapacitating me from my daily activities and from work. I was told after the surgery, by the surgeon, that I should be in bed and resting for the following three months, getting and sitting up for only a few moments at a time. Hahaha!!! Didn't I tell them I had to go back to work immediately? Well, after a few rounds of debate I was told that I should sit up, with the back brace, for only 30 minutes then rest supine for another hour or so. That was NOT going to work for me. I had to get back to my patients and clients after all, and pay the bills.

There were lessons to be learned from this pain and although I am nearly fully recovered now, at the time I needed a back brace, a walker, a cane and a lot of help. I now know the answers to my questions. Hopefully, it will help you too!

I needed to look back in time and find the source of my initial pain complaint. I wondered why the hospital I initially went to kept telling me the pain was from my hip even though I complained of sciatic pain down my right leg. It wasn't and after about nine months of getting nowhere with them that I finally went elsewhere for help.

I found that the sciatic pain was due to Spinal Stenosis in the L4 & L5 area of my spine, and it had become very severe over those nine months to the point that cortisone shots, acupuncture and physical therapy just wasn't helping. Neither was my own medicine. The doctor recommended minimally invasive surgery (and it was not). He didn't tell me what it would be like afterward only that I would need rest! That was the physical piece, but the spiritual piece became apparent when I discovered the loss that was consuming my life during those two years prior. It didn't matter that I was in pain. What mattered was dealing with the upcoming loss of residence, potential income and possibly my business.

I am spiritually fortunate and I am grateful. Yes, it would be a long recovery, but I am up and mobile now. Each day I looked forward to getting better and better so I could return to my yoga practice and walking in the woods. I did appreciate that I could still meditate, pray and see my patients (yesss!). I am using other holistic methods and a strict change in my diet (clean foods only) to help with my healing and a more rapid recovery.

The point? When you are doing soul work you have greater insight into an ailment or injury, whether physical or emotional. You also create a shift in perspective in dealing with and healing pain.

Spinal pain, especially in the lower lumbar is a message to us. If we think about it, the spine supports the whole body. When the lower spine causes pain and difficulty moving or walking it is telling us to slow down. It also tells us we have little or no supports. I also recognized that my Sacral Chakra was blocked as I had been going through some personal struggles leading up to this ailment. For pain in any part of the spine check to see which Chakra and organs it is connected to. This is how the spiritual is connected to the physical. More on Chakras later.

When I recognized this I had a sudden shift in my awareness about my life and what I was attempting to accomplish. I *saw*, from a divine perspective, the reason and purpose for having to move into my office space. I realized I did not have any supportive persons helping me with my admirable goals to expand my practice and include other holistic practitioners. I was adamant on moving forward with or without help regardless of what others' may have thought or said. "Stay where you are." You're doing great, just grow your own client base." That was not enough. Spirit had a mission to expand my practice so that the many people looking for holistic care could have easy access to it and to educate everyone on alternative and complimentary healing methods. This was instilled within me from a higher place. It became my Divine mission!

The pain, however, initially made me feel helpless and weak. Then I had another shift in awareness. The pain is helping me slow down, but it is also part of the healing process. I surrendered and welcomed the pain. I was healing in more ways than just the physical. It helps me to look within more often, to glimpse at the energetic fields around me and see how they are impressing upon my own energetic fields. All the work I have done for others I am using on myself: Organic Tuning, Acupressure, Reiki, Poultices, Alkaline diet, I'm even counseling myself and receiving counseling insights and inspirations during my meditative/contemplative time outs and my journeying.... I hope you're getting the picture.

I realized I was too focused on outcomes and am becoming more mindful of processing from a spiritual base. I am especially grateful to my one dearest friend who did come to my aid without asking. And another who helped in a very simple, but desperately needed way. Even a distant family member became a much needed helper. I realized, with my eyes open, I am not alone in my endeavors. Spirit has a way of inviting the gifts of others to present themselves if we are being aware enough to receive them and accept them as they are.

My message to you is to be mindful in your everyday life of those special little gifts that present themselves. If we can get out of our own way and tune in to what spirit guides us to do we cannot go wrong. Be in acceptance and open to receive. Pain, whether emotional or physical, can have a tendency to blind us to the miracles all around us. We just need to wake up to the beauty of life in all its forms.

Meditation or sitting in the silence was a major factor in my physical recovery and my emotional recovery. I really want you to know that this work is on-going for as long as we are still alive on this plane of existence. Don't let that deter you one bit! You are a soul. That is the state of being we are meant to be living even while in a physical body.

Remember, your sanctuary is your quiet space. A place where you can give yourself a time out. It will allow you to recover from your day, from all the tension and stress that you may be subject to.

Sit in the silence and allow your mind to drift away while your soul knowing becomes prevalent, leading, eventually to Divine mind. The same mind as that of Issa/Jesus, Buddha, Dalai Lama and many others. You have it within you already. You have had insights and intuitions throughout your life telling you there is something more. This is it!

*We cannot allow doubt to creep into our spiritual
consciousness. It may take some practice, but practice
makes perfect. Fake it 'til you make it. Be like an actor
rehearsing for a part and become the new
character. A shift in your consciousness
will take place sooner than you think
until the God within you is on
automatic pilot. Divinely guided at all
times we are provided and cared
or to our own highest good and the highest good of all concerned.*
Dr. Sandy Range

CHAPTER FIFTEEN

(C3) How Do I Get Rid of Ego?

This chapter, of course, relates to Chapter Three. We lose our ego by raising our consciousness to one of love. That may sound corny, but it means loving ourselves and our communities enough to create change and change begins from within. I love you, yes, you reader! I love this little blue planet and every living thing upon it (yes, even rocks, stones and dirt from the Earth are alive). I love myself as well. Do you love yourself? If not, you will need to learn how. That comes with letting go!

Every single person is experiencing an energy flux. This means we are going through a change whether we want to or not. Now, we can each suffer through the changes or we can be wide awake and in flow.

In order to love fully, and this means loving unconditionally we need to control our egos. Let me first begin with loving unconditionally. Many people don't quite know what this means or think it means having to love someone who is internally ugly (we don't like him or her). Loving unconditionally is tied to acceptance. When we are in acceptance of others, a situation, a condition, etc.

we simply accept them or it for who or what they are without making a judgement.

Really Angry People

What do you do when you are confronted by really angry people? They don't seem to understand the present moment and therefore remain in a state of anger and bitterness. I drove to Connecticut over a weekend and planned to stay for only one night. Down on Saturday and home on Sunday. My car sprung a transmission leak and I had to stay there until Monday needing to wait for the mechanic's shop to open and do the needed repairs.

Over the course of Saturday night, Sunday and Monday I stayed with a very good friend who was the house guest of another good friend. Both of them elders. Grandmother is 81 years old legally blind and an albino Native American. My other friend was a Medicine Man and just a couple of years older than myself. I love both of these elders dearly!

I partook of a much needed sweat lodge on Saturday only to be confronted with my car issue. I was not so concerned about it, but the woman grandmother calls her Hunka Sister (adopted into the family) became a rage monster. She complained that I was going to stay at Grandmother's house, she complained she had to wait for my tow truck to come. She complained about the sweat lodge and the people who attended. She complained about everything. I was just happy to get back to Grandmother's house while this woman went to hers.

On Sunday a barrage of people came through to see Grandmother and the Medicine Man, however he wasn't at home. So it was just me and Grandmother. I witnessed three different people come into her home and continue to tease, complain, and spew negative talk over and over. Each one was an anger monster. Each one's energy was thick and heavy with negative energies and emotions. It was difficult to sit in their presence. (With practice you will be able to feel, sense and even see other people's energies.)

When the angry woman (the Hunka sister) came in she told Grandmother to make her a cup of coffee. GM did and served it to her. GM then made the woman a cup of Buffalo Stew that I had made the night before for GM and the Medicine Man. This woman gobbled down two bowls full and then told GM to take the dishes away. Well, I had witnessed enough. This woman is in her fifties and GM in her eighties.

I did not confront the woman, but instead picked up everyone's dishes, brought them into the kitchen and washed them all. GM, however, asked me not to take them in as she would do it instead. I informed Grandmother that she is an elder and it is my responsibility to care for her in any way I could. That is the Indian way. GM smiled and sat back in her chair. The angry woman huffed and puffed and said, "She (GM) needs the exercise. I simply stated, "It looks like we could all use some exercise." She was a very big woman, but that was the only benign sarcastic statement I made.

As all of the people in the household continued to spew hate and bias and misinformation, I simply excused myself and asked if GM would like to come for a walk with me. The gentleman (and I use the term lightly) said, "Why are you taking GM away?" I replied, "Because it's just too toxic in here." Everyone in the room quieted down. One of the women became awake and said, "You're right. All we talk about is bulls#*t." I then stated, "GM deserves to be treated with respect, She needs to be honored. We all need to honor ourselves by shifting our consciousness and recognizing who we are as souls." I didn't hear another negative thing that day; not from any of them!

Sometimes, just small gestures and a single comment to the contrary of what is going on in the moment will wake people up and keep the anger monster at bay!

Here's what you can do to eliminate ego on a personal level:

- Love everyone and everything. Ego loves to sit in judgement, make complaints & hurtful statements and so much more. Love is the answer to putting ego in its place.

- Smile and greet others, even strangers, with a positive attitude and a hello. If they do not return the smile/hello, so be it! Keep smiling!

- Show kindness at all times. This is a magical practice as it prepares you for unconditional love.

- Give back or pay it forward. We all must learn to not only receive, but to give as well. When our vessel is full nothing can be added to it. When we empty our vessel by giving and doing for others, we have more room to receive blessings! The opposite is true for those who give their all and deplete themselves unable to receive. Learn to receive and create a balanced life.

- Surround yourself with healthy, positive people. There will come a time when you will need to end some relationships, whether family, friends or whomever. Surrounding yourself with like-minded people will assist you to elevate your own consciousness. We are here to learn and teach, teach and learn.

- Clear your mind and heart of negativity. This only weighs you down and keeps you in a perpetual state of hardship, struggle and strife. It can also cause physical illness over time.

- Plant seeds of wisdom in others. Everything you learn and practice you should pass it on. Help those you love to see things differently. When you come upon resistance simply plant the seed.

- Never argue with a closed mind. You cannot convince someone to think or see things the way you do, especially when embarking upon this path. Again, when met with resistance simply walk away with a smile.

- Present your very best self always, in all ways. This will be a work in progress for everyone. First, this doesn't mean you need to be perfect. It means to be who you are authentically and that is presenting yourself from the place of soul. Remember, be mindful!

- Think like a Creator. Think in terms of being Divine. You are. A creator is full with passion for life and beauty and love. Bring things into your world that are beautiful or beautify your soul.

- Bless everyone, even those you don't like or agree with. The art of Blessings is a powerful tool. It blesses both the giver and receiver. You can even send a silent blessing, but you must really mean it from your heart!

- Dismiss and rebuke any negative or derogatory thoughts or speech immediately. (Mindfulness) If, perchance, you happen to slip up and say something not so nice or even if you think something negative about someone or something, call it back immediately: "I rebuke that statement/thought and dissolve its power."

Here's what you can do on a societal & global level:

- Keep your neighborhood clean. Don't litter and pick up rubbish from the sidewalk.

- Grow your own organic food gardens. Create a community organic food garden.

- Use green fuels – solar and wind.

- Plant a tree or 2 or 3.

- Green your neighborhood with sidewalk or roadway native plant gardens.

- Use non-plastic, reusable water bottles. Recycle, reuse, repurpose.

- Use reusable bags in place of paper or plastic.

- Ask for and buy wood and paper products certified by the Forest Stewardship Council (FSC)

- Each One Teach One (and many more).

- Bless everyone and everything. Blessings have a way of healing and spreading.

You may ask, how does performing these acts eliminate ego? Well, doing all of these things allows your heart and mind to open and flourish. It is scientifically proven that when humans perform acts of kindness they are happier, more fulfilled, and are willing to do more. These are not the behaviors of ego.

Kindness and positive, healthy seed planting blesses the giver and the receiver. It can improve self-esteem and confidence without ego getting in the way. An article titled: *Prosocial Behavior Mitigates the Negative Effects of Stress in Everyday Life*, Elizabeth B. Raposa, Holly B. Laws, and Emily B. Ansell show how their findings suggest that "affiliative behavior may be an important component of coping with stress and indicate that engaging in prosocial behavior might be an effective strategy for reducing the impact of stress on emotional functioning..." So is it any wonder that once your mood elevates and improves your life does as well?

*"Connect with the core of your being.
That eternal flame of life that burns within.
Ignite the fire. Fan the flames."*
Dr. Sandy Range

CHAPTER SIXTEEN

(C4) Higher Mind to Divine mind

In order to develop the higher mind and flex its muscles we need to be still and silent. In the silence we can receive information. We must learn to ignore the rooftop chatter or "monkey mind" the Buddhists speak of. These are all the random thoughts that pass through our minds while we are usually silent. This happens while we are trying to go to sleep or when trying to practice meditation or just trying to have a little *alone by myself* time. Many people feel like they should eliminate all thoughts when meditating. This is not reality. At least not in this dimension of existence. We will always have these random thoughts passing through our minds. The trick is to acknowledge they are there and let them go.

Connecting to higher mind allows us to be able to purge old, outdated and useless behaviors connected to ego. Many of us carry the hurts and pains of childhood traumas or painful relationships or a loss of esteem and confidence. These can often result in a mental or emotional illness. If you must, because you are burdened with emotional or mental distress, please seek out a holistic therapist to help you. In this way you can free yourself from this daily burden that is holding you back from attaining your divinity.

How do we get there?

> - Gratitude! Lots and lots of gratitude. Be thankful for every little thing. Don't take anything for granted. Eyes open. Be mindful.

> - Treat everyone as you would like to be treated yourself. No one wants to be treated poorly. No one wants to be spoken to harshly. No one wants to be demeaned. Everyone wants to be treated with respect and so do you. Even your children deserve to be respected and treated with dignity! Never belittle them, especially in front of others big or small!

> - See everyone as a beautiful soul. They are and you are too. When you glance at another or look at another you are seeing another beautiful, luminous soul. That soul is priceless no matter how it may look on the outside.

> - Pay honor and respect to nature, to every sentient being, to all of life itself. You and the universe are one. You are made of the same substance inside and out. How are you more valuable than any other sentient being? This includes the plants, trees, animals, rivers & waterways, insects, winged ones, crawling ones and swimming ones!

> - Live your life impeccably (highest standards). Even your thoughts must be impeccable. It will take practice but you can master this. Because of our conditioning it's easy to slip into faulty thinking and speech. It's easy to slip into bad mouthing someone but we have to be mindful and call back any negative thoughts or speech we have let slip from our being. Call it back. Rebuke it. Deny it until it happens no more!

> - Resolve any and all conflicts you might have with family, friends, and colleagues. It's not worth harboring angry negative energy in your being. It's detrimental to your mental, emotional, spiritual and physical health. Most of our illness and sickness is caused by our mental distress and

negative, angry energy. We also expend much more energy being angry than when we are happy.

- Be mindful of faulty thinking in everything you do. Become aware of your outdated and useless conditioned thinking (remember the subconscious mind?) as opposed to your newly programmed healthy thinking.

- Living in the world through your higher mind helps to resolve negative karma, but that is not the reason you should practice higher mind. You must not have an agenda to do good. Do it because it's what is in your heart.

- Make a daily practice of sitting in the silence and repeating healthy, positive declarations and affirmations. You will create a statement and declare it, then you will repeat it over and over to affirm it. A declaration/affirmation might sound like: "I am grateful for and appreciate my family. I bless them and I am full of love for them." This is one I used to heal family conflicts and tension. It helped ME to release any judgements I had toward them and allowed me to simply be in acceptance.

I can't tell you at this time that I have reached a constant state of divine mind. I'm also unable to provide any case studies of any of my clients that have reached divine mind. What I can tell you is that I am very much living this life and walking through this world in a much higher state of consciousness than in many years past. As well, I have experienced times of living in Divine mind and it is beautiful! And many of my clients are also moving through the world from a higher state of consciousness. They are much more wide-awake, aware and alert than they have ever been, and all the happier for it.

You may think that practicing being in a state of Higher Mind is difficult. It is not. It is simply being mindful of your own thoughts, speech & behaviors. This is a good practice to have for any number of reasons, don't you think?

"Sometimes the road to success gets tough...really tough. You may consider quitting because it just seems too hard. Before you do, look back over your shoulder and see how far you've come. Every step, no matter how small, is progress! Keep on pushing on!"
Dr. Sandy Range

CHAPTER SEVENTEEN

(C7) The Road to Transformation

As you may notice, there are no *how to's* for chapters five and six. They're just not necessary, but I would suggest you go back and re-read those two chapters with an open mind. It just might help in your "transformation."

Let's speak a little about enlightenment again. To be enlightened is to be awake, aware, and in a state of gnosis. It is knowing who you are as a cosmic being and a soul! You are made of the same stuff as the stars, planets, moons and all other celestial cosmology.

I took an online course called, "Crack Your Egg" with "Henk Schram. Henk reports that science has shown us that our cells can be broken down beyond their nucleus. What did the scientists find? That our cells, when broken down into their protons, neutrons and electrons can be broken down even further into photons, quarks, neutrinos, etc.. They were further broken down to a discovery of them being *"entities of energy, scientists call quanta. And Quantum physicists believe that the entire universe is made up of quanta."* Henk also informs us that "two neurophysiologists at Berkeley" stated that the brain is a "frequency decoder."

So, if we think about our cells being pure energy without solidity at their base and only energy, we can understand how our bodies and everything else in the universe and on this planet is simply energy moving at various frequencies. When we recognize this we can allow the freedom and flow of the universe to merge with us. We can even heal our physical bodies. So, wouldn't it suffice to say that we possess the ability and the where with all to change ourselves and to shift our consciousness into a higher state of being?

Our thoughts are energy. Our bodies are energy. We can tune in to the frequencies we are resonating at and feel whether we are vibrating at a higher or lower frequency. Once we are able to feel our energy we can purposefully raise our vibrations through meditation, mindfulness and right living.

One other thing...Our thoughts are not the only things we have to be concerned and mindful about. Raising our consciousness to the level of higher mind and divine mind takes a holistic approach to include your mind, body, emotions and spirit. Let's look at some things you can do to get and stay healthy holistically:

Intentional Self's Daily Commandments to Help You Transform:

1) **Eat healthy to stay healthy.** I've been a vegetarian since I was 14 years old. I'm not telling you to stop eating meat/flesh, but if you did that would be very helpful. You can, however, purchase organic meats and eat it only 2-3 days a week. Eat clean foods, those not contaminated with GMO's, pesticides, growth hormones, antibiotics and goodness knows what else they feed and inject into these poor animals. Eat clean, fresh fruits and vegetables. Stop the fast food & junk food. It really does cloud the mind and cause illness in both body and mind.

2) **Get enough sleep.** At least 7 hours each night. Sleep is of the utmost importance. If you have trouble sleeping at night, whether difficulty falling asleep or waking up during

the night or both, get help! Set a regular schedule for when to go to sleep and when to wake up and stick to that schedule no matter what. Even on the weekends! This is what the National Sleep Foundation says to do: "Stick to a schedule; practice a relaxing bedtime ritual; avoid naps in the afternoon; evaluate your room and keep the temperature between 60 and 69 degrees…"

3) **Clear your mind & heart of other people's stuff.** When we hold onto things said or done, we are the only ones suffering because of it. The incident no longer exists. It is in the past. We hold negative emotions inside us and carry around all of that feeling. Why??? Let it go. It no longer exists. The only one hurting is you. The other person has most likely moved on, or the situation/circumstance has passed and is now history. Find your freedom in the moment with a clear mind.

4) **Surround yourself with healthy, positive thinking people.** Healthy people are mostly happy people. They are inspired, always moving forward, always looking to make things better in their personal lives and in the world. These people are the ones you want to surround yourself with. Try connecting with someone who inspires you in positive, healthy ways.

5) **Behave as if you are the world's role model.** Think about the legacy you will leave behind when you are gone. How would you like people to remember you? What are you doing to make the world a better place? Even just your positive attitude and smile can make a difference in someone's life. Remember, each person we meet is a luminous soul, just like you! Behave accordingly!

6) **Stay in the present moment.** It's the only reality there is. The present moment is where things happen. It is where you make changes and begin new ventures. When our thoughts are always thinking of some past event or situation, or when thinking about the future we are unable to be fully present in the moment. As well, we are NOT fully living. Life can

only be enjoyed in the now time. The future is good to think about, but only when we are planning for it in the moment.

7) **Find your joy and hold on tight**. When we embark on this work we eventually find joy! Some people have never experienced joy, but I'll tell you what – go back in time to when you were a small child. Remember playing all by yourself or with other friends. See yourself laughing hysterically and moving your body. Remember how that felt! Remember the freedom of just being you and having a great time. Children naturally know joy until their parents or caregivers squash it out of them! Find that joy again and hold on tight!

8) **Do something each day toward achieving your dreams.** When we are busy with designing, or building our future we become exhilarated. When our plans get put into action, even if it's only the first step we feel a sense of accomplishment. When we do something each day toward our practice of enlightenment we get better and better at it!

9) **Take time out for you.** Replenish and Rejuvenate. Self-care is of the utmost importance in this work. If you are not taking care of your complete self, you will struggle through life, may become ill over and over and live with brain fog. Take 15 minutes each day to meditate. Remember to be mindful with everything you do throughout the day. Make the right choices. Speak the right words, etc.

Take time outs from your daily grind. Go for a walk, stand outside and look up at the sky, practice yoga, breathe deeply. If you can get away, then get away! Remember, nature is your best friend!

10) **Don't waste a minute of your life!** Live it Fully! Spiritual work is not a solemn, isolating, silent experience. It is honoring the life force within us and living fully.

11) **Pray with sincerity.** Brent Secunda, shaman and healer, and founder of the Dance of the Deer Foundation says of prayer: "The Huichol [people of Mexico] say that by praying to the "Ancient Ones" and the spirits of the land, we build a relationship with nature. Pray daily, with positive intentions, and your prayers will be heard."
12) Help Heall the Planet. You can help hela the planet with a few simple changes. Recycle; stop buying plastic and items wrapped in plastic; don't litter and if you do, pick it up and dispose of it properly; be mindful of your utility usage especially the fossil fuels. It may be hard to not use them right now, but we need to push for more alternative energies. It's difficult right now for many of us to go completely green and purchase a new electric vehicle or place solar panels on our rooves, however, we can be mindful of how much utilities we are using and find ways to cut down on our consumption.

*"Connect with the core of your being.
That eternal flame of life that burns within.
Ignite the fire. Fan the flames."*
Dr. Sandy Range

CHAPTER EIGHTEEN

(C9) I Thought I was Already Authentic!

No, I didn't forget to add Chapter Eight here. That chapter has its own lessons built in. There is nothing more I can say. So, let's begin with Chapter Nine, Authenticity.

Being Authentic is being your true self as we stated previously. How do I find my true self? How do I know if I am being my true self? But, I'm already being my true self and if you don't like it, too bad!

Hmm! For those who think they may already be living their authentic selves I commend you. But if you think that you are I would suggest giving yourself and ego-check! Do you feel pride in your authenticity? Do you attempt to correct others in their spiritual practices? Do you feel you know all there is to know? I would suggest you practice more gratitude and humility.

In my own spiritual work I still need to practice humility. I need to check my ego every day! As long as we are living on this earth plane we are ruled by our egos. They are not that easy to contain, but can be contained and controlled!

Okay...authenticity is being authentic. It is being genuine, real, originally you, but if you haven't already lived as a soul in your human body, you are not being your authentic self. Let's see if we can find a path to becoming you authentic self.

> Learn to Sit in the Silence. This practice assists one to go within to seek and commune with the Source of All That Is.

> How Do I Sit in the Silence? Mindfulness & Meditation. Remember, in mindfulness we are fully present in the very moment. This means we tune out all distractions, other people's chatter, noises from TV, radio, PC/laptop, and anything that may cause us to become distracted away from the present moment. Make it a practice to be mindful in every moment of every day. This practice will help with your meditation as you sit in the silence.

> Set Up Your Meditation Space. Do you remember how to set up your meditation space? Create a small (or large) space in your home or office where you will not be disturbed. Place a small table, a soft lamp or other diffused lighting. Place objects that have spiritual meaning to you (it doesn't have to be a lot. 1 or 2 will suffice). Place a picture, statue, flowers, etc. You may want to burn oils or incense for the sacred aromas they provide and will put you in the mood. You will need a Meditation cushion or a comfortable chair with a straight back. Make your space beautiful for you. Paint the walls (if allowed), hang beautifully colored fabrics or add a nice area rug. This is your space for your inner work! Do not allow anyone in there unless they too are meditating.

> Make Meditation a Daily Practice. Meditation is the art of going within and developing concentration and focus. It is a method for learning how the minds works in its own patterns and habits. It allows one to see the self as it truly is in all its colors, dark and light. It allow us to know what must

stay and what must leave us. It is the mirror to our finger pointing. It is the path to our enlightenment. Meditation is the quintessential path to God and the God-Self within.

➢ But How Do I Practice Meditation? There are many techniques that people use to meditate. Following are some of the most recommended and easiest to use:

1) Go to your prepared meditation space. Light your candle, incense and whatever else you need to make your space sacred to you!

2) Sit comfortably. Release all the tension and stress of the day through your breath.

3) Begin breathing with an exhale, then take a slow, long deep breath through your nose for the count of seven. Hold for a count of three. Exhale slowly for a count of seven through your mouth with the tip of your tongue touching the roof of your mouth. Relax. This technique was taught to me by my maestro, Don Oscar Miro Quesada of Heart of the Healer.

4) As you inhale, imagine all the light of the Universe entering through the top of your head, filling you up completely. As you exhale, imagine all the toxins, tension and stress leaving through your heart center.

5) Keep your peace and just breathe normally

6) Focus on your breath. What does it feel like, as you Inhale, going into your nostrils? Cool, difficult, easy. Can you feel it going down into your lungs? What does it feel like? What sensations are you getting?

What does your exhale feel like? Is it warm? Can you feel it as it exits your lungs and nostrils? What is your body feeling as you breathe in this rhythmic fashion?

7) Relax – Breathe – Sit in the Silence. When any thoughts begin to enter, just notice them and let them pass. Don't

choose one to focus on. Bring your focus back to your breath. In time and with practice the thoughts will become lighter and less intrusive.

You will find your authentic self through this practice. You will also recognize when ego is trying to take control. The more you stay in the moment (mindfulness) the more your true self (soul) will be in control over ego. Once you recognize that you are soul and not your gender, age, name, job or whatever else that is outside of you, you will understand the true meaning of authentic self.

You might also set an intention for your meditation. Bring into focus something you desire, need to accomplish, learn, etc. Only focus on question and not the how. The Universe will provide the how.

"It is now time to stop placing blame & time to take responsibility. We can continue to moan & groan & complain about everything we do not have and cannot do in life! It is time to look at the role WE have played in our OWN struggles. Take a good look at SELF! Take Ownership! Make the necessary changes!"
Dr. Sandy Range

CHAPTER NINETEEN

(C10): Finding the Meaning

Finding the meaning for everything in our lives depends on your consciousness and its elevation. This means unless we are in or at a state of elevated consciousness or thinking, we will continue to create meaning that is hurtful or harmful to us. We harm ourselves by creating meaning that is self-sabotaging: "I lost my job because I'm stupid." "My wife left me because I'm not good enough for her." Do you get the idea?

When we can see with better eyes, we see the true meaning of our lives. The above self-sabotaging statements could be very different: I lost my job because the company is downsizing and I am newly hired. I got a better job. This is a blessings!" or "My wife left me because she was cheating on me and I can't be with a woman like that." This kind of Meaning Making opens the door for better things to walk in.

At the same time, we need to be mindful about ego getting in the way. Ego is the culprit that is always there, ready to pounce and keep your life in the status quo of turmoil, stress and chaos. Go back to chapter three and re-read about the ego.

Remember in chapter ten we spoke about delusional human beings of two kinds? Which one are you? Do you have delusions of grandeur or of insignificance? Are you the center of the Universe or do you hide away always fearful of something? Either way it is ego that produces this state of consciousness. Either way you hurt yourself.

You hurt yourself when playing too big. Others will begin to fade away from you unless your ego has control issues as well. Then you will attempt and succeed in controlling others. This does not issue good karma and in fact, will produce residual effect karma that you will pay for one way or another. When you play too small and hide away from life you diminish your light. You might allow others to manipulate you; maybe you can't find your voice and are unable to speak up for yourself. Playing small like this also issues you a karma ticket. You live this life over and over until you shine your light and love yourself as a co-creator. Make some meaning of your life now. Once you've done the work of clearing and healing you can begin to live a conscious, meaningful life going forward.

Meaning Making is a method for self-reflection, healing and release. It is helpful to follow this process:

➢ Take time out for self-reflection. You can meditate to bring in mindfulness of your life's history.

➢ Go back in time and see who you may have hurt in the past. This is about who YOU hurt, not who hurt you. If it was both ways that's fine, just continue the process.

➢ See the person, animal, being, place, or circumstance. Once clearly in your awareness, see what you did in all honesty and truth. You must be truthful. You are only working with yourself so no room for lies or make believe.

- Then see how it could have played out differently, without harm and with a positive & healthy outcome. Use your imagination.

- Once you have the healthy outcome hold the person, being or circumstance in your consciousness and embrace him/her/it. Ask for forgiveness and mean it from your very soul.

- Wait until you feel the negative energies from that event to leave you and be replaced with feelings of love and release.

- Be aware of your emotional states during this process. Try to name what you are feeling: anger, sadness, embarrassment, shame, hurt, pain, or anything else? It is good to name or identify your feelings so they do not become internalized. Acknowledge the feeling then let it go.

- Before engaging in any activity or communication, remember to wait until all emotional states have passed from you and you are feeling light, loving, and clear.

- It is also very important to be mindful of your ego. Be sure that ego is not doing the forgiving. If it is no forgiveness actually happens and you are just going through the motions.

"Take care to feed your body, mind and
spirit with only those things that
are pure, good and healthy. Reject impure
foods, thoughts and behaviors.
Remove the toxins that poison your Being within and without.
Do this now and live a life of longevity and divine purpose, for
you will be honoring your most Sacred Self and the Creator."
Dr. Sandy Range

CHAPTER TWENTY

(C11) Healthy Habits Maintained

First I would like to inform you about the many Indigenous cultures around the world that still utilize their original medicine and treatments that come from the earth and from Spirit.

I believe it is time to return to our cultural origins and practice the old ways. These ways are not archaic, religious, blasphemous or devil worship. They are traditional methods for healing illness of the mind, body and spirit. These practices have been around since the beginning of humankind on this planet.

As I said in an earlier chapter, if you are not caring for and healing the whole of you (mind, body, emotions and soul), you will never be completely healed. Think about it, if you have all of these constitutions within and because everything is connected, why would healing only one part of you make you whole? The mind, soul, body connection is strong. It is one organism with many parts. You must address the whole of you to be completely healed.

There are many Indigenous cultures around the world that view certain mental illness as Spirit awakening, a Shaman within!

> Research and Read about Malidoma Patrice Some', a West African Psychologist and how he came to visit a psychiatric ward in a mental hospital in New York City. He reported that the patient's he saw screaming and crying in the ward were the reactions of a spiritual warrior (shaman, healer, medicine person) trying to get free and at the same time being chemically suppressed by pharmaceutical drugs. Dr. Some' states these patients only need guidance and a teacher to set them on the path.

It is only in the West that hearing voices and seeing visions is a mental illness like Schizophrenia. Think about it. Do you pray? Do you talk to God, your guardian angels or even your ancestors? Then you are talking to spirits. Do you hear their voices speaking to you? Do you get insights and inspirations when you pray or meditate? That is Spirit speaking to you. Are you Schizophrenic? No!

What is really important right now is for you to find out who you are at your core. Try this little exercise:

- ➢ Get a journal and write down all your beliefs and values (take your time. Really think about it).

- ➢ Once you know your beliefs and values, go over your list and ~~strike out~~ all those beliefs and values that were never yours, but maybe instilled in you or that you adopted as a child from parents, caregivers, teachers, friends and others.

- ➢ Write a new list of your own true core beliefs and values. What is unique and different about the real you?

We all, as human beings, have a responsibility. We all carry our essence (soul) into the future. We have received information for this lifetime from our ancestors, even though they may not have been healed yet. But we also are the guide for our descendants, whether by blood or community, to follow us. What will you teach them? Will they know who they truly are?

Times are changing and we need to learn to live on this beautiful planet in a manner of peace and harmony. We need to embrace our eco system and promote its growth and good health. Without returning our planet in her healthy state, all living beings will perish. In *The Book of Ceremony*, Sandra Ingerman says:

> ...everything that exists on the planet is connected to a web of life. You can think of this web like your body. You are made up of multiple organs and cells, each of which affects your health, and each of which is impacted by your words, thoughts and energy. In the same way the web of life is a weaving of living creatures who all contribute to, are impacted by, and are energetically reshaped by our intentions, thoughts, words, daydreams and states of consciousness.

This is why it is so very important to make the change within ourselves; to raise our states of consciousness, to use all of our God-given senses to see with better eyes, hear with better ears, speak with kinder words, feel with heart, touch with tenderness, Taste the sweetness of Life! You can create all of this in your life. You can soar above the craziness and take others with you. Remember, plant those seeds wherever you go.

There is another issue we should discuss. This is intergenerational trauma. We spoke above about how we inherit from our ancestors and leave parts of us to our descendants. The shamans of Peru have given a specific name to these traumatic conditions passed down to us by our parents, grandparents and ancestors. Dr. Alberto Villoldo, Ph.D. is a psychologist and Peruvian shaman. He states in his new book, *Grow a New Body*:

Psychological themes run in families, passed down from parent to child…In the Amazon, they call this a generational curse. When left unacknowledged and unhealed, it can trigger heart disease or cancer. Autoimmune diseases, which involve the immune system attacking our own cells, often run in families with poor emotional boundaries–where individuals have trouble acknowledging what is yours and what is theirs… The childhood fears, anger, suffering, and feelings of abandonment encoded in our neural networks cause us to repeat the underlying themes of these memories, even if we don't recall the events themselves. And this is what it means to have a generational curse; you keep repeating family patterns which wind up showing themselves as illness in the body and mind.

We already have everything we need within us to heal ourselves. First – Get your soul right. Soul is the one thing we tend to ignore. Soul is who we truly are. This body is simply the vehicle. It is the temporary home for the soul to reside. In a previous chapter I asked, *Who is the thinker of your thoughts?* You may answer, "Me." But who is me? You are not your body. You are not your brain. The brain is simply an organ I like to relate to it as the computer server, the headquarters that keeps the body running. It is Brain Mind that ego is attached to and it is part of the Brain stem. The primitive part of our brains that relate to fight, flight or freeze. Can you recognize your patterns of behavior when you're out and about? Can you recognize your reactions and thoughts to other people and situations? Pay attention. Be mindful of those thoughts, feelings and reactions. Are they calm and peaceful or are they negatively reactive? If the latter, you have work to do, but you are now on the path.

*"Our Ancestors are our relatives that came before us.
They need to know we are thinking of them.
They will also help us heal the traumas of the past.
Make your ancestors feel loved. Communicate often."*
Dr. Sandy Range

CHAPTER TWENTY ONE

(C12) The Ancestor Connection

I do hope you read chapter twelve and understand the importance of making a connection with our ancestors. Whether we know it or not we are guided by the legacies our ancestors left behind. Most times we look to our most recently transitioned ancestors to try and understand why we behave and think the way we do, but they are not healed yet. And they still carry all of the baggage they had when they were still with us.

There is a process all transitioned souls go through once they are on the other side. They need time to review their lives and because they are pure soul now, they do not have the attachment to what has happened to them in their most recent life, but they may still carry the residual effects of that life. That is what each one needs to work out and heal.

Sometimes when a soul has had an extremely violent and or hostile life, being a perpetrator, they will often be taken to a place where they are resolved of the energies of that life. They will still need to review and work on their healing. Some of those souls will return and fall right back into the same patterns as the previous life.

This is why it is important for each one of us to live our lives impeccably. To live in a way that is conducive to soul growth and evolution while we are still here. It is so important to wake up, eyes and hearts open. Living from the heart center instead of our heads (ego). When we learn to evolve in this life, we evolve in the next. Listen to your ancestors, they will help you.

Now, to learn a little about how you can connect with your ancestors. You may want to sit with someone who knows how to work with the ancestors before you begin your journey. A learned person in this work will help to keep you from any entities you don't want coming into your environment. That person can also teach you how to protect yourself. Okay, here we go:

1) Create an Ancestor Altar. This can be a small table. Place a nice covering over it. Place photos of your ancestors on the altar. Place a candle and other objects they maybe belonged to them. You can also place objects that have a significant or spiritual meaning for you. Light an incense. Place a sugar skull if you're inclined to do so.

2) Sit with your altar and meditate on your ancestors. Talk to them. Call for the ones who are healed and whole. Just be quiet and listen. Pay attention to your senses. What do you feel or sense around you? What do you smell or see in your mind's eye? Sometimes they will come very gently and sometimes they come very strongly.

3) You can also add a despacho with some food and flowers for them. You will need a medicine person or shaman to show you how. But you can leave bowls of their favorite foods on your ancestor altar. They love sweets too! And don't forget the water. They will need a cup of water on their altar. You only need small bowls of food like dried fruits, jerky, any kind of side dishes they liked. Make it healthy! These are all offerings that make our ancestors happy.

4) Once you are done with your food for the ancestors you will need to take it outside and either bury it or wash it away in flowing water (a river, stream ocean, etc.)

These are all ways we can make connection with our ancestors. Even if you don't have a picture you can envision them in your mind's eye, even if you don't know what they looked like. Allow spirit to take over and communicate with them in a deeply revered way. They are always here for us and will help us if we ask. I would suggest getting to know who they are first. Establish a relationship with them. Them you can ask them for advice, information and insight into your life issues. Have fun with them, but be respectful. They love you!

The Illumined Ones!
The Ones who were sent to earth to shine our Light.
We are the Ones who will heal humanity.
The Ones who are doing good for others.
We are the Illumined Ones.
We vibrate at a higher frequency.
We see with better eyes. Hear with better ears.
We face all challenges as moments of learning.
We continue to grow and evolve.
We do what is right and rebuke negativity.
We are the Illumined Ones.
Let us Re-Member!
Let us hold true to our cosmic nature.
Let us walk through the world as One.
We are all the same. Just our Avatars look different.
We are the Illumined Ones!
Dr. Sandy Range

PART THREE

YOUR BEGINNING

"Remember...YOU are the LIGHT! Shine Brightly! Be Beautiful!"
Dr. Sandy Range

CHAPTER TWENTY TWO

This is the Beginning

This chapter will provide information to add to your Spiritual Awakening repertoire. It contains different subjects and information, but it all relates back to the content provided in this book.

You must get ego under control, even to a degree where you are mindful of every time it shows up. Yes, this is a repeating pattern throughout this book because it is at the core of how to heal and remove all of our negative karma and repair ourselves. Once ego is in check we begin to see the world differently.

In an interview with Oprah Winfrey in the June 2006 issue of O Magazine, actor Hugh Jackman reports of ego: "The ego says, 'you don't need to meditate, man. You're really busy. What about the kids?' But do I say, I can't shower today because I have to make time for the kids? No."

This is what we all need to do. We will always make excuses to separate ourselves from our spiritual work. This is why we suffer throughout our lives. Now, it doesn't matter how old or young you are, you must take up this path. If the lessons in this book are not for you, then find someone or something that will teach you or train you in the truth about our human/spiritual constitution.

When people are driven by ego in their lives they become paranoid and controlling, and in severe cases, delusional. People are so mistrusting of others that they actually believe they are always unsafe and have a need to find and incriminate an innocent bystander and protect themselves in extraordinarily nonsensical ways. Do you watch the news? There you have it. I'm not saying there are no real dangers in the world, but when we elevate ourselves it's like having a force field around you. Your energy just doesn't attract those things. However, you may have some karmic events that need healing and releasing.

If you practice the exercises in this book you will become an enlightened one. Your consciousness will elevate and your energetic frequencies will vibrate at a much higher rate. Maintain a healthy, clean foods diet, exercise, or just take a daily walk. See others for the Soul they truly are and respond accordingly. Spend time in nature.

Yes! Make time to be in nature! Nature is our cure all for emotional, mental and spiritual chaos and disruption. We can even heal physically walking or being in nature. You might try finding a Medicine Person, Healer, or Shaman to help you through any tough conditions.

Practice finding beauty in all things everywhere. You can even see beauty in a crumpled up piece of paper. Look with your spirit eyes and see its colors, shadows, dimensions. Beauty can be found everywhere. Take your shoes off and walk on the natural earth to ground yourself to Pachamama (Mother Earth) and receive her energies in return. A good practice is whenever you are feeling depressed, angry, anxious, sad or whatever, go outside barefoot and stomp the ground for about two minutes with the intent to have all those toxic feelings and energies drain out through the soles of your feet into the earth to be transformed. Then just stay grounded by walking the ground until you feel better. I do this whenever I can, but in Massachusetts we have quite a few months of cold and snow on the ground, but I do walk barefoot in the house.

This was a miraculous technique when I was in New Mexico with my Yuwipi man. During sweat lodge there was a man who made fun of everything this Lakota Yuwipi Man taught them all week. During this sweat a spirit came in and possessed him. He began to shake violently. The men on the other side held him down so he would not be burned by the hot rocks in the lodge. The Yuwipi had to move quickly to remove the spirit from this man. As he did he motioned for me to hold a place my fingers on his shoulder (a meridian point). As I did I immediately felt a jolt run through my entire body. The woman next to me felt it rush through her legs as we were touching knee to knee. Later that night after the sweat I continued to hold the energy of that spirit. The Yuwipi said. Go outside and pound the earth with your feet. I did for about an hour before that energy left me. I love you Pachamama!

Now, I want to speak a little about death. We will all leave this planet someday. We don't know when or how, but we will definitely go. Most people don't like to think about death, especially their own deaths. But are you prepared to die? Most people, when asked to get their affairs in order, think they must hire a lawyer and make a will, pay off all debts, let people know what you want for a funeral, burial or cremation. Well... there's more to getting your affairs in order than just your bills! You have to Get Your Soul Right!

Make the practices in this book part of your life. Find beauty in simple things. Accept others as they are. Acceptance in all things is liberation from the tyranny of the ego. When we avoid the truth, when we are indifferent to it we become or remain anxious and fearful. Fear drives all of our negative emotions and their reactions. The moment you can treat everyone as equals, you will worry less about who might be offended or not.

We should be prepared for our deaths. Begin by resolving all of your conflicts with others and yourself. Break those ties you have with toxic people. You are actually breaking the thought that binds you to them. Understand this and unburden yourself. Do all of the suggestions and practices in the previous chapters to the best of your ability. In this way you are cleaning out all energies that are harmful and toxic. You are clearing your mind and your thoughts. Your elevated vibrational frequencies and consciousness will allow you to pass from this life with acceptance, love and dignity, knowing you are a Divine being and have nothing to worry about. Be sure to help educate your family members and loved ones about your spiritual journey into Divine mind and also be sure to teach them now before your time comes.

Spiritually awakened people deliver love and care to self, their surroundings and the global community. We understand that we are all One. We understand that everything is connected and that whatever we do, think, and say has an energetic reaction. Spiritually awakened people walk through the world softly. They walk the Red Road path. In Indigenous America many tribes practice walking the Red Road. Remember that from chapter seven?

So, the Red Road speaks about how to live in the world. The description I provided provides proof that most indigenous cultures know how to live in and with the world. However, due to Western influences, many traditional cultures are losing their sacred medicine and ways of life. But there are those who are trying to protect the teachings, medicines and even language of many indigenous peoples around the world. Let's help keep the flame burning by accepting that there is more than Western medicine and thought to heal us in much healthier ways.

We are so used to the darkness of this world and our society it's hard to awaken to the light. It takes time and effort. We can stay asleep in Maya (illusion) or we can wake ourselves up and out of our self-imposed prisons. In the Hindu scriptures, "Samadhi, which literally means 'to direct together,' is the state in which a yogi perceive the identity of his soul as spirit. It is an experience of divine ecstasy as well as of superconscious perception; the soul perceives the entire universe." (Ananda. Web). This is true and I have experienced Samadhi once in my lifetime. My practice is to get there again and stay there.

Stop competing with your friends and colleagues. Women, stop competing with other women. Men, stop competing with other men. People, stop competing with each other period. It's just not necessary and causes more harm than good on both parts. Instead, lift each other up. Lend a hand, pay a compliment or open a door. When you help others succeed, you succeed and you open a pathway for abundance in your own life. You are also rising above and showing others how to do this work without them even knowing, but they will feel the energetic shift. Just be mindful of ego getting in the way of your good works!

We must begin to live our lives in a higher state. It begins with you and me. Each on teach one. This is a Sacred Journey that heals us as human beings both inside and out. When we are healed and whole the planet gets happy!

We really need to understand the sacredness of life: human life, animal life, plant & mineral life, insect life. The lives of the elements: water is life, air is life, earth is life, fire is life, ether is life. Without any of these life will perish. Every single one is sacred and dependent on the others for survival. Yes, we human beings are dependent on the earth, its creatures and the elements for our survival. It's time we began to pay attention to the destruction we are causing to our dear and sacred Pachamama or Mother Earth. We kill Pachamama, we kill ourselves.

I am very passionate about nature and our sweet mother who nourishes us all. I care deeply about our environment, all the plants, trees and animals. We are all One after all. Even in my home and my office I have allowed spider people to live with me in their corners. I once had a spider in a basement studio apartment for 3 years. It had grown from a tiny speck to about one and a half inches. It was huge. No one noticed it was there and I loved that it would eat all the other creepy crawlers I didn't want around. One day my best friend came to visit. I was in the other room and I heard WHAM! Of course the noise got my attention and she came running in to tell me she had just killed a big spider over my front door. I was heartbroken and devastated. Spidey had been my pet for three years. My friend did learn a lesson as well. When she saw my reaction, I explained to her what the spider was as a spirit and what it meant to be a sentient being. I have had many insect visitors over the decades even a little leaf legged bug from Peru that arrived in a package from there. He or she was beautiful! I will never kill a sentient being. If there is a creature that should not live in my home, I speak to as I would a friend and ask it to leave my home and that this place is not conducive to its' life. It usually will leave thereafter. If not, I find a tissue or other object to remove it safely, keeping it alive and well!

Make your life a ceremony in everything you do. We all have our own personal rituals we practice every day, from brushing out teeth to stopping at that favorite coffee shop for that morning java. Ceremony can be made more special by incorporating your daily practices from this book in a reverential and sacred manner. Sandra Ingerman, in her recent release, *The Book of Ceremony (2018)* states: "Ceremony brings the sacred into ordinary life...Performing ceremonies creates a bridge between the material world we live in and the world of the unseen, the divine, the power of the universe…."

So, besides the techniques I have given you previously, please work on your soul self with diligence. When you leave your home in the morning or whenever, greet the day with a smile and gratitude. Give thanks for every little thing in your life. We need to express our appreciation for everything we have animate and inanimate. Gratitude for all the little things that happen to us throughout the day. Maybe someone smiled at you on the bus, or the checkout girl found and gave you a discount you didn't expect. There are many ways that we are blessed by life all the time. We just need to open and see with our god-eyes and our hearts to see them and appreciate them.

Moving through the world with an open heart may seem an impossible task. Since the world is so crazy and our society appears to be getting sicker energetically you might think that opening your heart will cause you pain or get you in trouble. It won't. This is the medicine we need. It is what our society needs and what our earth needs. I can't emphasize this enough.

When we open our hearts we become Soul. When we become Soul we empathize more, we feel more compassion, we feel happier, we don't sweat the small stuff or even the big stuff. We just deal with it and move past it. And those challenges that arise will always be dealt with in a state of higher consciousness so we are not feeling the pains and struggles internally as we once did. Go back to Chapter One about "change." An open heart and a higher consciousness allows us to move through the world almost effortlessly. Challenges become our life-college professors teaching us about ourselves and how we manage our affairs. Spirit always has the answers. We just need to tap into this information and receive the blessings that await us.

"The next time you feel down, blue or
sad try a little Play Therapy!
Yes, it's good for adults too!
Try a role play; look in the mirror and laugh a lot;
get on the floor and roll around; play tag/
hide & seek with some friends;
hang from some jungle gym bars;
play any of the games you played as a
kid or just have fun & be silly!"
Dr. Sandy Range

CHAPTER TWENTY THREE

You are the Universe. The Universe is You

About Affirmations

The affirmations on the next page are some of those I use myself. Here is a starter for you. Add your own and/or tweak what you see here. When speaking your affirmations, hold the intent and emotion for each one. Re-member your heart must be open. When your heart is closed you are unable to receive. Women have a tendency to give, give, give and never receive. If your cup is empty, man or woman, open your heart and allow the fullness of the Sacred to fill you and your life. Re-member, you must keep the balance of giving and receiving. Repeat your affirmations with devotion and from your heart center. Not your head!

It is so important that we be mindful of getting out of our heads and into our heart centers. As an example, when two people who speak different languages meet and feel an affinity for one another, they can understand what the other is trying to communicate because they are coming from their heart space. We can communicate with adults, children and animals the same way without using language.

The heart will always speak more clearly and accurately than the mind's language.

The heart is our truth. When we listen to our hearts we understand a situation better. We also come from a loving space so that all is open to healing and comfort. Emotion, when used properly, is the core of manifesting what we need for our lives. The emotion of love heals everything. Love yourself, love others, love the world. Affirmations are strong multipliers of energy. Feel them as you speak them.

MY GIFT TO YOU – FILL IN THE BLANKS

1. I AM Creator's vessel to uplift, inspire, heal, and promote wellness and prosperity in every way to everyone. I bless this gift.
2. I appreciate and love all the joy, happiness and love that permeate my life. I bless this gift.
3. I AM a magnet for my (soul mate, career success, like-minded friends, etc.) _____ that prosper my life. I bless this gift.
4. I AM grateful for and appreciate my family. I bless them and I AM full of love for them.
5. Every day I grow and evolve for the better and for good. I bless my mind, my spirit and my body.
6. I AM a powerful and successful _____. I bless this gift.
7. I AM full with appreciation for my good health, fit body and long life. I bless this gift.
8. I AM thankful to live in luxury with the freedom to live an abundantly healthy and wealthy lifestyle. I bless my homes, my land, my cars, my bank accounts.
9. I AM humbled and thankful that I can share my wealth where and how it is needed most. I bless this gift.
10. I AM grateful for my abundantly successful and financially prosperous _____.

I have perfect gratitude, thankfulness and appreciation for All That Is.
I Bless All That Is. I Bless the Realization and
Manifestation of ALL I Desire.
I Bless the Year 20__
The Ineffable Great Parent and the Universe provide me joy, happiness, infinite and abundant wealth, treasures and blessings each and every day! And each day I am prospered more than the day before.
MANIFEST ~ MANIFEST ~ MANIFEST
© 2019 Dr. Sandy Range

We can heal the body, mind and spirit through energy healing. Is that really a thing? Well, yes, it is a thing, a very potent thing.

Energy healing is usually done through the hands of a healer. What most people don't understand is that it is not the person administering the healing, but the flow of energy being channeled through the person.

This energy is something that each of us possesses, but may not know or understand how to tap into it or channel it for good works.

This energy is sometimes considered Divine energy, Universal energy, Cosmic energy and God energy. This energy is all around us all the time. Most people, however, are oblivious to it. Really good energy healers practice diligently. Most will meditate day and night to commune with this divine source of energy. There are those who are mindful and devoted to the practice of mantras, chants, singing, yoga, prayer, dance, sweat lodge and other methods of connecting with the Divine Source. One purpose for this is to raise his or her consciousness so that she/he is automatically guided by spirit. When this happens the strength and power of Divine healing energy can be quite powerful.

Not only does the practitioner commune with the Energy Source, the practitioner uses concentrated thought to connect and channel the energy. The practitioner will direct his/her focus on the hands as the tool of God's healing energy and light. Therefore, this Divine energy source flows through the practitioner, the conduit or open channel, and through his or her hands. This energy then flows into the area of the body needing healing connecting with the recipients own God energy.

There are many types of energy healing and most have been around for thousands of years both in the East, and in the West with Indigenous cultures. Western minds are really just getting into the swing of things because many have seen and felt the benefits of energy healing. Below are just a few.

All energy healing modalities can be done just as powerfully without actually touching the body and can even be sent long distance. This is a good choice for those who may have been traumatized or sexually assaulted/abused. Energy healing with body manipulation may include Massage, Shiatzu, Acupuncture, Acupressure, Bioenergy Healing, EFT or Tapping. There is so much more out there these days.

Always check to see if your practitioner is experienced, knowledgeable, and in most cases certified or licensed to practice.

Alternative Therapies

There are so many holistic and alternative therapies out in the world right now there is bound to be a few you could or should try! There's Sound therapy. Light therapy, Yoga, Guided Imagery/Visualization, Aromatherapy, Essential Oils for bathing, Acupuncture, Ayurveda and so much more. Then there is your diet to keep your body clean and pure. Research what clean foods are and incorporate them into your daily meals. Research and find the right organic herbs, vitamins and supplements to take to help your body heal, energize and vitalize. There are even herbs & supplements to help with mood and anxiety. Go the natural route, but do your research and ask a professional before purchasing off the shelf. Find an outdoor activity you can engage in even if it's just walking in nature.

Johrei

Originating from Japan Johrei has Seven Spiritual Principles of the Universe incorporated by the Johrei Fellowship are: 1) Order 2) Gratitude 3) Purification 4) Spiritual Affinity 5) Cause and Effect 6)

Spiritual Precedes the Physical 7) Oneness of the Spiritual and the Physical. Johrei is very similar to Reiki, also from Japan.

Pranic Healing

Prana is the life force and is sometimes referred to as breath. There are two principles at work in Pranic Healing. 1) Life force, energy or Qi allows the body an innate ability to heal itself. Even with surgery, medications and other medical model practices, the body always heals itself. When no healing occurs the body no longer has life. 2) The sources of prana may come from the foods we eat, but also from the elements like earth, sun, water, air. It can come from other people and from sources of spirit. www,pranichealing.net

Wouldn't it suffice to say that if we maintain a healthy lifestyle, both inner and outer, we can command our bodies to heal themselves? We still may need a medical doctor, but we will heal more wuickly and organically if we engage in pranic healing.

Restorative Touch

Restorative Touch™ is a type of energy healing that works on a resonance of the recipient's own highest potential, calibrating and aligning their body and field to that highest potential. Practitioners work mostly with their hands in the client's energy field.

Bioenergetic Healing

Wilhelm Reich, a psychoanalyst, founded Bioenergetic Therapy and further developed by his student, Alexander Lowen. Bioenergetics assists in healing the stress and tensions that build up in the body that may be due to traumas, and other mental and emotional conditions.

Emotional Freedom Technique/Tapping

EFT Tapping is based on Chinese Medicine and the meridian points used in acupuncture and acupressure. The meridians are the pathways of energy in the human body. Tapping these meridian points helps to restore balance in the body and can even work on the emotions. It is believed that tapping the meridian points signals the brain to control stressors and restore balance to interrupted energy flow.

Reiki Healing

Reiki has been very westernized over the decades, but is a very useful tool for spiritual and energetic cleansing and healing. It is a Japanese technique that trains the Reiki practitioner to be a vessel for the energies throughout the universe to be routed directly to the client by laying on of hands. Reiki works with the Chakras. Chakra healing is something many people don't know enough about. The Chakras are energy center in our bodies. There are seven primary chakras attached to the physical body and more to our spiritual bodies, twelve in all. They begin at the very base of the spinal cord.

This is the Root Chakra. Then you have the Sacral Chakra located just below the navel. The Third Chakra is the Solar Plexus located at the diaphragm, just below the ribcage. Next is the Heart Chakra located in the heart. The Throat Chakra locate in the throat. The Third Eye Chakra located in the center of the forehead slightly above the eyebrows.

The Crown Chakra is located at the crown of the head. One more Chakra is the Soul Star located a few feet above the head.

The Chakras are like little vortexes that spin out from our bodies from the front and the back. They can become out of balance or blocked completely. This can be the cause of many ailments, emotional, mental and physical. If you feel like you are have difficulties in your life, go see a good Reiki practitioner.

Healing Through Sound

"Music without words means leaving behind the mind. And leaving behind the mind is meditation. Meditation returns you to the source. And the source of all is sound." **Kabir**

This is a very profound statement! If you're a regular meditator then you know about the vibration and frequency of sound waves. The sound "OM" or "AUM" is said to be the sound of creation, and when chanted correctly the sound of AUM made through the voice causes vibrational frequencies throughout the body that can actually loosen blockages and assist in healing. The same can be said for other forms of Sound and there are quite a few: voice, musical instruments, tuning forks, Singing Bowls, drums, the wind, animals, all things in nature...you get the idea!

There are a few particular sound instruments used frequently for Sound Therapies. Below is just a small sample of the more common ones, but there are a whole lot more: *I love my drum circles!*

Drumming, for instance, can cause a trance like state where one might feel removed from the body. The first sound we hear while still in the womb is the sound of the mother's heart beat drumming rhythmically, soothing us effortlessly. Drumming resonates with our body's natural rhythms and helps to synchronize the movement of the organs and the flow of our life force, the blood. It creates mindfulness while deepening internal awareness. Studies have shown that drumming lowers both blood pressure and stress hormones, induces a meditative and relaxed mental state that reduce anxiety and tension, activates both sides of the brain and can help the mind achieve hemispheric coordination. Drumming combined with deep breathing and visualization techniques offers even more stress reduction benefits. Drumming is grounding and fun. Drumming groups are becoming very popular and you don't even need to know how!

Tuning Forks are very significant in assisting to loosen and release blockages, balance bodily energies and frequencies and promote healing. They are made to create very specific frequencies of vibration and sound to produce different results: Solfeggio Frequencies use six tones. The Six Solfeggio tones include: UT – 396 Hz – Liberating Guilt and Fear; RE – 417 Hz – Undoing Situations and Facilitating Change; MI – 528 Hz – Transformation and Miracles (DNA Repair); FA – 639 Hz – Connecting/Relationships; SOL – 741 Hz – Expression/Solutions; LA – 852 Hz – Awakening Intuition. The traditional Pythagorian scale or chakra frequencies from the Hindu tradition use a full middle octave of eight tuning forks (C, D, E, F, G, A, B, C) with C being the root chakra, D the sacral chakra, etc. The tuning forks emanate pure sounds and overtones to help you relax and center yourself. The vibrations fill you inside and out – providing a soothing and deep healing sound bath.

Himalayan Singing Bowls are another force of nature! The tones, resonance and vibrations differ from Himalayan bowls and crystal bowls. Crystal Bowls are made from silicone glass, and produce what is scientifically called a pure sine tone. Sine tone is one pure, intense tone as opposed to the complex interweaving of three sets of double tones, rich in harmonics and microtones produced by the Himalayan singing bowls. Most people find that the Himalayan singing bowls have a mellower feel compared to the intense tones of the crystal bowls. The tones of Himalayan singing bowls and are thought to synchronize sentient brain waves and create a therapeutic effect on the mind and body. Science stands behind the effects of therapeutic sound. Dr. David Simon, medical director of the Deepak Chopra center in California, found that sound vibrations from Himalayan bowls and chanting are chemically metabolized into "endogenous opiates." These substances act on the body as internal painkillers and healing opiates.

The commonalities of all of these sound therapies: Energizes the body, soothes and balances the nervous system, lifts the spirit, Promotes an almost instantaneous deep state of relaxation, deepens a meditative state, improves mental clarity, enhances brain functioning, increases mental concentration, centers and balances the body, balances and integrate both sides of the brain, balances and realigns the chakras, clears and charges the aura, clears and raises vibrational frequency, promotes healing of body, mind and emotions.

A WORD ABOUT LIGHTWORKERS OR ENERGYWORKERS

There has always been a great debate as to whether Lightworkers (people engaged in teaching or practicing Spiritual & Healing works) should charge for their services. After all, it is "spiritual" isn't it? I have heard time and time again that "spiritual workers" shouldn't charge for this work.

Many Christians believe so because they believe Jesus gave away his teachings and healings for free…or did he? What we do know about Jesus is that his disciples would collect money, food, wine, clothing and secure shelter for Jesus and His crew as they traveled throughout the Middle East. Sufi tradition says *never* give away spiritual knowledge. They believed that there must be an exchange.

Those who pay for their Spiritual classes, groups or services are more appreciative, have a sincere interest, and want to learn grow and evolve.

At Intentional Self we had attempted to allow participants who were too depleted financially to come to our groups and services for a very low, discounted price or for free. Yes! We thought we were doing a great service for these folks! However, what we discovered was that the people who paid a low or no fee for services would show up late, not understand the content, be agitated during the service, would become very noisy and generally caused unrest for the entire group or class.

What many people do not understand is that Spiritual Practitioners or Lightworkers also have to pay rent or mortgage, have utilities to pay, car notes, insurance, shop for groceries and clothing, and…well, you know what it costs to live in today's society.

There is a great value to spiritual and holistic knowledge. Those who seek this knowledge should remember that those who provide the knowledge may have spent many years or decades studying and practicing. They have spent countless hours and dollars learning their practice and keeping their certifications, and/or knowledge up to date.

These practitioners, the Lightworkers do this first out of love: love of how the knowing and practice assists in elevating the mind, body and soul; and a love for sharing what they have learned and what they know. Spiritual practitioners, lightworkers and teachers desire for every human being to grow and evolve and become something better and exceedingly enlightened. This is what they offer the world.

If you know a lightworker please, show them respect and honor their gifts, because without lightworkers our planet would be much, much darker, filled with much more pain and suffering!

Hypnosis/Hypnotherapy

Hypnotherapy is another useful tool in removing outdated subconscious habits that keep us stuck. Think of an iceberg. The twenty percent above the water is your conscious mind. The eighty percent below the water is your subconscious mind. Your subconscious is the warehouse or storehouse of all of your experiences, learnings, information received, lessons learned (good and bad), since birth. This is what the conscious mind uses for information on a daily basis. Imagine what you are carrying as an information highway to move through your life. A great deal may not be serving you well. Go find a hypnotherapist to help you purge all the outdated and useless information you've been living by.

Psychotherapy

In some cases you may need to find a holistic or spiritual psychotherapist to help you move what is really stuck within you. A psychotherapist is trained in various techniques to help you realize what is keeping you stuck and move past it then heal it (holistic/spiritual counselor). Your counselor will also keep whatever you tell him/her in strict confidence. He or she is an objective, outside person you can talk to without judgement or criticism. There is *no* shame in seeking help when needed.

Diet & Lifestyle

When we begin to cleanse and heal and live from the heart center and be the soul that we are, we need to engage in a lifestyle that promotes our spiritual work. I don't mean running off to the Himalayas or becoming a recluse. It just means being thoughtful, mindful and creating beauty all around us, especially in our personal surroundings. It also means paying attention to our diets. If you must eat meat, please eat only organic meats not pumped full of toxins and chemicals and GMO feed. Eat organic if you can. It is only expensive if you think your body will stay healthy all of your life while eating fast foods and junk foods. Organic vegetables and fruits are high on the list. Do you know what those little four and five digit numbers are on your veggies? Find out! They tell you what is organic, what is traditionally grown and what is GMO. Create a lifestyle for yourself that reflects your inner light and vibrational frequency.

Shamanism or Medicine Work

If you can find a learned Shaman or Medicine Person (always check out their lineage and practice) these people can heal you and teach you how to get back to nature and natural healing. Shamanism is the oldest medicine practice on earth. Many people are returning to the old ways and this is one of them. They can also help with your ancestor work, and many other spiritual issues. Shamans work with nature, spirits, and plants, among other things in their work.

There's Magic in the Air!

What is Magic? It is *not* Satanism or any other evil debauchery. Magic can happen anywhere and at any time with a little effort! Basically, magic is in the eye and heart of the beholder! Sometimes we see magic in something beautiful and majestic. Sometimes we witness a magical event. And sometimes we cause magic to happen! Just think about it. I'll bet you've experienced or witnessed magic at one time or other in your life!

Magic can be as simple as pure, uninterrupted mindfulness or it can be profound. Everyone has used magic at some point in time. You may have thought about something so hard for so long while working toward an end goal to produce something magical in your life. Or maybe you work to heal others with your hands and heart and witnessed a miracle (magic). Maybe you see something wonderful and magical in someone else that no else can see!

We need more magic in our lives. We need to look at the world with childlike innocence and see magic everywhere! We need to bring forth our creative powers to manifest more beauty, wonder, joy and love! Everyone possess magic. It is in your heart and soul. Do magic by being magical! Open your eyes really wide and take in the beauty around you! Send a blessing. Make a wish. Change a life. Life is really m-a-g-i-c-a-l!!!

Begin Sweet Soul

My desire is that we change, heal and uplift every human being, one person at a time. If every person shed their old, ego ridden clothes (energetically) and allowed Soul to shine and show forth there will be no wars, no violence, no poverty, no sickness. The world and all its creatures will thrive because enlightened people will be managing it. We so desperately need this right now.

==Strive for your Divine mind, your Enlightened Consciousness. Be the Light. Be the Change. You are Light in human form. You are the Cosmos in action on earth.== You are the Universe with all its intelligence at your disposal because the Universe is you and you are the Universe.

Walk the path slowly. Don't worry whether you are progressing or not, unless you are not actually doing the work. Take your time. Follow the steps in this book that feel comfortable to you. Practice and practice even more. Practice makes perfect. You will become the Light that you already are in human form. You will be a beacon for others to emulate. Again, take it slow and find a practice, like mindfulness, that you can practice daily. Then take on one more and one more until you've mastered them all.

Remember, the whole purpose of these practices is to help you to grow and evolve mentally, physically, emotionally and spiritually. We need to remember that we are Divine Beings in human form. If we are mindful of this fact we will grow exponentially in our pursuits of evolution.

To you my reader. Thank you for supporting my work. May you be comforted in the warmth of spirit, wrapped in a cocoon of gnosis and freed from the slavery of ego. Thank you beautiful Soul! Many Blessings and Much Munay!

RESOURCES

Credible News Sources from Forbes Online – 02/21/2017

Paul Glader is an associate professor of journalism at The King's College in New York City, a media scholar at The Berlin School of Creative Leadership.

1. The New York Times

This is the most influential newspaper in the U.S. in my view. Its editorial page and some of its news coverage take a left-leaning, progressive view of the world. But the NYT also hews to ethical standards of reporting and the classic elements of journalism in America. That's what helps the NYT remain, arguably, the agenda-setting news organization in America. It is a leader in business, politics and culture coverage. *

2. The Wall Street Journal

The largest circulation newspaper in the U.S., the *WSJ* made its bones as a business newspaper and pioneered new types of feature writing in American journalism (for example, its quirky middle-column feature called the "Ahed" and longer form, in-depth reports called "leders"). As the company was purchased by Australian media mogul Rupert Murdoch in 2007, the *WSJ* pivoted to cover more general news in addition to business news. The *WSJ* is still brand X among daily business publications in the world. Its editorial page is a bastion of American free-market conservatism, using the motto, "free markets, free people." With former Republican speechwriters and strategists such as Karl Rove, Peggy Noonan and Bill McGurn writing columns, the *WSJ* editorial page is often a must-read for Republicans in Washington. And left-leaning readers should not dismiss the *WSJ* edit page just because they may disagree with its positions. It has won several Pulitzer Prizes for editorials and columns that feature a clear thesis, backed up by thorough fact-based reporting and bold arguments. *

3. The Washington Post

The newspaper that brought down President Richard Nixon with its reporting on the Watergate scandal in the early 1970s maintains its intellectually robust tradition under the new ownership of Amazon. com founder Jeff Bezos. The *Post* has, for decades, been part of the big three national papers – a peer of the *NYT* and *WSJ* – in terms of winning Pulitzer Prizes, hiring the best and brightest reporters and producing big scoops. Of the big three, the *Post* is arguably the most forward-thinking right now in trying new digital strategies that have boosted readership. And with Bezos' backing, the *Post* is on a hiring binge for talented reporters while the *NYT* and *WSJ* have been pruning their reporting staffs in recent months. Most people think the *Post* editorial page leans left but is often regarded as more center left than the *NYT*. *

4. BBC

The BBC is the global standard bearer for excellence in broadcast radio and TV journalism. If only U.S. cable news outlets could follow BBC's recipe. And while PBS produces some great entertainment, documentary and news programs, its news programs have often seemed to lack the creative energy of the BBC. While NPR produces some fantastic journalism, a bulk of its news coverage seem to come from re-reporting news from the *New York Times* and the *Associated Press*. And the American public perceives NPR to be more left-leaning than the BBC.

5. The Economist

Another British export, the Economist magazine is staffed with excellent economists and journalists who produce a tightly-edited, factually rigorous account of what's happening in the world each week. One oddity is that theEconomist doesn't publish bylines of their writers so you never know who exactly wrote a given piece.

6. The New Yorker

This American treasure publishes sophisticated narrative non-fiction pieces from top writers and reporters each week in a print magazine and, increasingly, on other platforms. The *New Yorker* is smartly expanding its audience on the web, offering to the masses content that used to be open only to its print subscribers. The magazine itself runs a piece of fiction each week (identifies it as such). The long-form non-fiction reports on politics, culture, business and other topics often take months to report, write and fact check. The result is deep reporting and analysis each week that is hard to find elsewhere. And the narrative structures and techniques the writers use make for enjoyable reading. Similar to the *Times*, the *New Yorker*presents a progressive view of the world. Conservative readers should recognize that but not let it detract from them enjoying some of the best reporting and writing happening in the world. *

7. Wire Services: The Associated Press, Reuters, Bloomberg News

You can't exactly "subscribe" to these wire services. But you can trust reports from these organizations to be factual. They provide a backbone of news and information flows about politics and the economy. And their member organizations that surface their reports benefit from this reporting. You can follow these organizations on social media and can also follow certain reporters for these organizations who report on topics of interest to you. These wire services also do have web sites and mobile apps you can use to stay abreast the news. *

8. Foreign Affairs

This bi-monthly magazine is published by the Council on Foreign Relations. It's a serious magazine for people who want intelligence on global affairs. The magazine and its many digital platforms benefits from submissions, dialogue, differing views and analysis from the many top minds on international relations.

9. The Atlantic

This is another national treasure, a monthly magazine that presents a view of the nation and world from Washington D.C. It is informed by many top journalists who write long-form features and also write some analysis. The *Atlantic* web site sometimes hews to clickable headlines. But the magazine and its parent company also subscribe to American journalism principles of fact-based reporting.

10. Politico

Founded by reporters who left the *Washington Post in 2006, Politico* has built itself into a crucial player in politics reporting in the U.S. (and with expansions to Europe). It does publish some products in print, but *Politico*is easily accessible on the Internet and mobile devices. Keep an eye on Axios, a news startup launched this year by two founders of *Politico*.

Runners Up:

- National Public Radio
- *TIME* magazine
- The Christian Science Monitor
- *The Los Angeles Times* (and many other regional, metropolitan daily newspapers)
- *USA Today*
- CNN
- NBC News
- CBS News
- ABC News

Business News Sources:

- *FORBES* magazine
- *Bloomberg BusinessWeek* magazine
- *Fortune* magazine
- *The Financial Times* newspaper

Sources of reporting and opinion from the right of the political spectrum:

- *National Review*
- *The Weekly Standard*

Sources of reporting and opinion from the left of the political spectrum:

- *The New Republic*
- *The Nation*

Positive/Good News Sources:

The Optimist Daily: https://www.optimistdaily.com/
The Daily KOS: https://www.dailykos.com/
The Daily Good: http://www.dailygood.org/
The DoDo: https://www.thedodo.com/
The Good News Network: https://www.goodnewsnetwork.org/
Positive News: https://www.positive.news/
Yes Magazine: https://www.yesmagazine.org/

Page 18: PCU Codes for Fruits and Vegetables

https://www.consumerreports.org/cro/news/2010/05/what-do-plu-codes-say-about-your-produce/index.htm

WORKS CITED

Ananda. Excerpt on Samadhi. Web.

Besant, Annie. Esoteric Christianity or the Lesser Mysteries. Quest Books. Second Edition. Theosophical Publishing House. 2006.

Bidstrup, Scott. Strobel, Lee. The Case Against "The Case for Christ" A Study in Christian Apologetics. Web.

Boston College School of Theology. "Profile: The Gospel of Matthew." Web

Branco, Raul.The Pistis Sophia: An Introduction. Originally printed in the fall 2011 issue of Quest magazine.Citation: Branco, Raul. "The Pistis Sophia:

An Introduction." Quest 99.4 (FALL 2011):144-151.

Bible, King James. Syndics of the Cambridge University Press. Luke 2:47; Matthew 2:23.

Cirlot, J. E., A Dictionary of Symbols. Taylor & Francis e-Library, 2001.

Desaulniers, Veronique, Ph. D. How Emotional Trauma Can Create Cancer. Web.

Early Church. History of the Early Church. Irenaeus. Web.

Forest Stewardship Council (FSC). Web

Gnostic Church of L.V.X.,The. Sequence of Aeons. Web

Groothuis, Douglas. The Gnostic Gospels: Are They Authentic? Part Two. Christian Resource Institute. Web.

Holy Bible, The. Mark1:9. Holy Trinity Edition. The Catholic Press, Inc. Chicago, Illinois.

Ingerman, Sandra. Book of Ceremony. Sounds True. 2018.

Jackman, Hugh. O Magazine. Interview with Oprah Winfrey. June 2006.

Kabot-Zinn, Jon. Mindfulness CD. https://www.mindfulnesscds.com/

McFadden, John Joe Ph.D. Making the Quantum Leap. School of Biomedical And Life Sciences University of Surrey. UK.

Meyer, Marvin. The Nag Hammadi Scriptures. The Revised and Updated Translation of Sacred Gnostic Texts. The International Edition. 2007. Harper Collins Publishers.

Mead, G.R.S., Pistis Sophia: The Gnostic Tradition of Mary Magdalene, Yeshua and His Disciples. Lexington Kentucky. 2016, Oxford Dictionary. Web.

Miro-Quesada, Don Oscar. Heart of the Healer. 2018

National Sleep Foundation. Web.

Pagels, Elaine H. Gnostics and Other Heretics. Article for PBS. org. Web.

Pockett, Susan. The Nature of Consciousness. Writers Club Press. 2000.

Pranic Healing. Pranichealing.net. web.

Ramacharaka, Yogi. Mystic Christianity. The Inner Teachings of the Master.

Rough Draft Publishing. 2012.

Raposa, Elizabeth B., Laws, Holly B., Ansell, Emily B. Prosocial Behavior Mitigates the Negative Effects of Stress in Everyday Life. Journal Publications. Web

Rumi

Schram, Henk. Crack Your Egg. Crack Your Egg Enterprises, LLC. Web Training publication 2018.

Secunda, Brent. Dance of the Deer Foundation. Article. 2019

Simon, Dr. David. Deepak Chopra Center.

Some', Malidoma Patrice. West African Psychologist and Shaman.

Titleman, Gregory. Random House Dictionary of Popular Proverbs and Sayings" Random House, New York, 1996.

Villoldo, Alberto. Grow a New Body. Hay House Inc. 2019.

Yogananda, Paramahansa The Autopbiography of a Yogi. Self-Realization

Fellowship; Reprint edition. January 5, 1998.

Wikipedia. Web.

APPENDIX

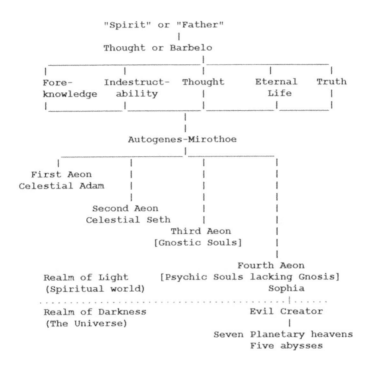

"This early Sethian text describes the sequence of Aeons; being but a secondarily Christianized work. . . .based on the early chapters of Genesis and as a revelation as given by the resurrected Christ to John, the son of Zebedee. . ." (The Gnostic Church of L.V.X.)

ALPHABETICAL LIST OF OLD TESTAMENT AUTHORS PART 1

- Amos: The book of Amos
- Daniel: The book of Daniel
- David: Psalms (Other authors wrote portions of Psalms as well)
- Ezekiel: The book of Ezekiel
- Ezra: The book of Ezra (Additionally Ezra is thought to have written 1st and 2nd Chronicles and possibly portions of Nehemiah)
- Habakkuk: The book of Habakkuk
- Haggai: The book of Haggai
- Hosea: The book of Hosea
- Isaiah: The book of Isaiah
- Jeremiah: 1st and 2nd Kings, Lamentations, the book of Jeremiah
- Joel: The book of Joel
- Jonah: The book of Jonah
- Joshua: The book of Joshua
- Malachi: The book of Malachi
- Micah: The book of Micah
- Moses: Genesis, Exodus, Leviticus, Numbers, Deuteronomy (Moses possibly compiled/wrote the book of Job)
- Nahum: The book of Nahum
- Nehemiah: The book of Nehemiah

- Obadiah: The book of Obadiah
- Samuel: (Samuel is believed to have written 1st and 2nd Samuel, Ruth, and Judges)
- Solomon: Ecclesiastes, Proverbs, Song of Solomon (also known as Song of Songs)
- Zechariah: The book of Zechariah
- Zephaniah: The book of Zephaniah

The Gnostic Church of L.V.X.

ALPHABETICAL LIST OF NEW TESTAMENT AUTHORS PART 2

- James: The book of James
- John: Gospel of John, 1st John, 2nd John, 3rd John, Revelation
- Jude: Book of Jude
- Luke: Gospel of Luke, Acts of the Apostles
- Mark: Gospel of Mark
- Matthew: Gospel of Matthew
- Paul: Romans, 1st and 2nd Corinthians, Galatians, Ephesians, Philippians, Colossians, 1st and 2nd Thessalonians, 1st and 2nd Timothy, Titus, Philemon (possibly the book of Hebrews)
- Peter: 1st and 2nd Peter

The Gnostic Church of L.V.X.

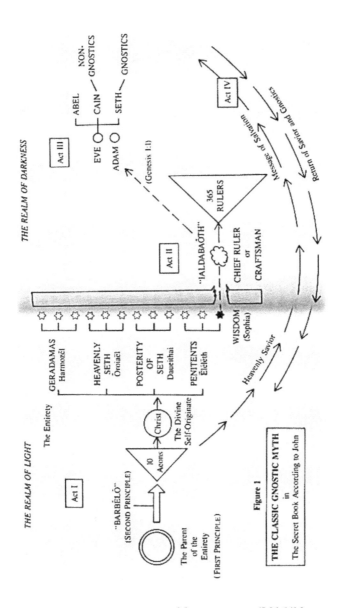

Figure 1

THE CLASSIC GNOSTIC MYTH in The Secret Book According to John

CPSIA information can be obtained
at www.ICGtesting.com
Printed in the USA
BVHW030947280719
554512BV00001B/111/P